Dear Boys

THE LETTER EVERY
SON NEEDS FROM
HIS FATHER

Dustin Kaehr

Copyright © 2018

All rights reserved. No part of this publication may be reproduced, stored in a retrieval system, or transmitted in any form or by any means—electronic, mechanical, photocopy, recording, or any other—except for brief quotations in printed reviews, without prior permission of the author.

ISBN: 978-0-9973541-3-3 (sc)
ISBN: 978-0-9973541-2-6 (eb)

Edited by Susan Chilton (www.susanchilton.com)
Cover design by Katie Pearce (www.pearce.media)
Cover photo by John Tirotta (tirottaphoto.smugmug.com)
Author photo by Brooke Miller
Interior design by Kim Monteforte (WeMakeBooks.ca)

Bulk discounts are available for your company, church, or non-profit for reselling, gifts, or study groups. For information or to have Dustin speak to your conference, church or retreat, reach out to *hello@dearboysbook.com* or find Dustin on Facebook, Instagram, LinkedIn, or Twitter (@dustinkaehr).

Printed in Canada

For My Dad, Scott Kaehr
(07.03.56 – 12.16.09)

In showing me how to die,
you showed me how to live.

Table of Contents

THE SET-UP

Start Here..................................	3
The Gettysburg Address.....................	9
Your Challenge..............................	21

THE LETTER

Sentence One: Your Guide.....................	43
Sentence Two: Your Mom......................	59
Sentence Three: Your Manhood................	75
Sentence Four: Your Guides...................	103
Sentence Five: Your Job......................	117
Sentences Six & Seven: Your Wife..............	133
Sentences Eight & Nine: Your Savior...........	151
Sentence Ten: Your Reminder..................	167

YOUR TURN

Your Turn To Write...........................	177

"When you teach your son, you teach your son's son."
THE TALMUD

The Set-Up

Start Here

I need to start here: I am a follower of Jesus Christ. He has been my Savior since I was 14 years old. My faith journey has had many ups and downs. I do not claim to have it all together or to have all the answers. Nevertheless, this book is written through the filter of that worldview and my personal relationship with Jesus. I know that only through my choice to follow Him will I have any chance to raise my four boys into great men. I am much too flawed to do that on my own.

But whether you are a Christ-follower, a casual Christian, or of no faith at all, I believe this book will help you raise your sons. The strong desire to raise our boys into men who love their wives and who are themselves great dads is not unique to me because of my relationship with Jesus.

As a dad, the one thing we all should want for our sons is that they grow up knowing how much we love them, how proud of them we are, and that we have prepared them well to go into the world.

Some credit for this book must go to bestselling author, Mark Sanborn. Back in January 2011, I was listening to Mark share the importance of clear, concise, effective communication. Because my mind tends to wander (sometimes farther and faster than it should), I began to apply what Mark was sharing, but to something completely different.

That five-minute daydream prompted me to begin writing on the plane ride home. Those musings eventually ended up on a blog I had at the time. When I started writing this book, I once again found myself in a daydream, but this time of my own doing. I have always enjoyed writing and joked for several years that I was going to write a book.[1] Well, in this second daydream, I became convinced that it was time to pick up a pen—or get behind a keyboard. As I began to ponder what subject I wanted to tackle, I was drawn back to that Mark Sanborn keynote about clear, concise, effective communication.

As a father to four boys, nothing could be more important than making sure that if something were to happen to me before my boys were raised, my message to them would be communicated in a way that would take root and be permanently entrenched in their hearts. For the sake of my wife, my boys, their future wives, my friends who are raising boys, and dads everywhere, nothing could be more important.

If you are a father, nothing is more important than the lasting messages we leave and model for our sons. I hope you read my story and apply it to your own journey.

Using This Book as Dad

I have designed this book so you can go through it with your son. There are some really simple questions at the end of each chapter for you two to answer together. My hope is you will read a chapter, have your son read it, and then go to breakfast and answer the questions. To work best, your son probably needs to be at least 13 to answer the questions in a meaningful way. As Dad, the best training he can get is to hear you share the answers to the questions and why those answers are important to you.

---

[1] After I started writing this book, I did write and publish a business book so, technically, this is the first book I ever started to write and the second one I have published.

Through your answers, he will hear what being a man sounds like and, in your actions, he will see how a man acts.

As you answer the questions, I encourage you to be honest with him. If the answer to the question is going to make you look bad, so be it. He needs to see you vulnerable. He needs to see you admit it when you fall short. He needs to see you work to correct things that need correcting.

Raising boys into men does not just happen. It is a process and there has to be intentionality (more about that word later). My hope is that this book provides that for you.

When my sons turn 13, I take them out to breakfast and share my definition of Manhood with them. I tell them that over the next three years, I want them to watch me as I model that definition. I tell them they will hear me recite the definition a lot as I raise them and discipline them. The definition becomes foundational for them and me. Honestly, the definition is something all my boys hear me repeat regularly. I work it into as many conversations as possible.

I embarked on this book for selfish reasons. Even if I hadn't published it—and, now, if no one buys it—it does not matter. I plan to spend a year walking each of my sons through this book. They will get a copy when they turn 15 and by the time they turn 16, we will have been through all of the chapters.[2] Then, on their 16th birthdays, I will give them a handwritten letter from me asking them to join me in living as Godly men.

(At the back of the book, there is a guide to helping you write your own 10-sentence letter to your son. I hope that by the time you reach it, you not only understand why you need to do so, but

---

[2]Don't worry, I will probably sell them a copy at a discount.

also have the confidence to do so.)

If you have other men in your life, I encourage you to call on them as you go through the book. Have a brother, uncle, grandfather or friend help lead your son through a chapter. If you know a group of dads and sons, you can all go through it together. You will appreciate the support of other dads and the boys will learn the importance of openly exploring life together.

Use this book as much or as little as you want as you raise your boys. Use it just as I have laid it out. Change it to fit what you are doing. Use it only as a reference. The fact that you are willing to read this and do *something* with your boys means you are doing more than most fathers, so thank you!

However you proceed, share your journey with other dads who are doing the same thing! Let's use the power of social media to encourage and support each other. When you go to breakfast with your son, post a picture, and use #dearboysbook.[3]

Using This Book as Son

If your dad has given you a copy of this book, let me tell you what I already know about you: You are loved. The fact that your dad is making the effort to go through this with you tells me he cares very, very deeply for you. No, this book won't help him dress more fashionably or put an end to the dumb dad jokes, but what it will do is bring you and your dad closer together.

As you read, know I am writing to your dad. But I also want you to take the thoughts and ideas and do a few things. First, compare them to what you are seeing lived out in your dad's life.

---

[3] If you still think the "#" is the pound sign, ask your son to help you!

I promise I am going to challenge him and make him squirm a bit. Enjoy that. But also encourage him where you see him doing well.

Second, think of yourself as grown man who is married and has two kids (a son and a daughter). Take the thoughts in this book and remind your future self of the absolute importance of getting that right.

Finally, there will be questions at the end of every chapter for you to answer, too. Here is your chance to think deeply and respond. Do not just give one-word answers. Challenge your dad's answers; don't let him off the hook if you think he's going easy on himself.

Oh, and since he's buying, order the biggest breakfast you can.

One Final Thought

Some of you may read this book and think, "I wish I had read this earlier!" An old Chinese proverb says, "The best time to plant a tree is 20 years ago. The second best time is today."

I want you to know it is never too late. Whether your son is eight or 58, it is never too late to open up or express regrets or write him a letter such as the one we work toward.

I promise, regardless of his age, your son will appreciate it, cherish it and be changed because of it!

So will you.

The Gettysburg Address

A righteous man who walks in his integrity—how blessed are his sons after him.

PROVERBS 20:7
THE BIBLE, NEW AMERICAN
STANDARD BIBLE

Sons are a heritage from the Lord, children a reward from him. Like arrows in the hands of a warrior are the sons born in one's youth. Blessed is the man whose quiver is full of them.

PSALMS 127:3-5
THE BIBLE,
NEW INTERNATIONAL
VERSION

Dad

The title "Dad" is one of the highest honors ever given to me. Next to serving my Savior and loving my wife, it is my highest calling. Knowing I am responsible to guide my sons as they become all that God has called them to be is exciting, humbling, overwhelming, and scary—all at the same time. It is something that, given too much time to think about it, seems to be a task for which I am ill-prepared, under-qualified, and destined to fail. There is no doubt that being Dad is a journey of walking (sometimes crawling), not running. Add to that the weight of being responsible to lead, protect, and care for the family and nothing short of panic can set in.

That is why this book is so important to me. It is my way of planning for the future. It is my way of guiding my boys into Manhood at all costs, above all else. It is setting a foundation and example for them that, by the grace of God, will impact my grandsons, great-grandsons, and beyond. This message, when communicated and executed correctly, is an absolute game-changer. It is a message that has been in my heart since the moment I held our first son in my arms, yet has taken over a decade to express.

Go back to the first time you held your child in your arms. Can you remember what you thought as you gazed down at that newly breathing, tiny, completely dependent human? It really is hard to put into words. But I believe that wrapped up in a jumble of thoughts and emotions is the idea of, "Oh man. Now what?"

We begin to process all the ways our lives just changed. In what should be the happiest of moments, we even allow ourselves to worry about how we will pay for college. We ask questions like, "Just how much is car insurance for a 16-year old boy?"[1] We question every decision we have ever made and wonder if we have what it takes to raise this little person into a well-adjusted, "normal" adult. The responsibility of "Dad" presses in on us almost immediately and we pray for the strength and wisdom to live up to this daunting mission. Nevertheless, as our boys begin to grow, we settle into a routine with them and we simply resume life.

Then, as our boys get older, we begin to have this nagging question: "How am I going to help my son become a man?" I know it is my job to call my boys into Manhood. However, in order to do that, I have to know what I am even calling them *to*. I mean, "What does it *mean* to be a man?"

Without a clear understanding for myself, I have no chance of guiding them. This would be Exhibit A in the blind leading the blind.

For me, an answer was being formed before I even asked the question. My journey started with Pastor Robert Lewis's *Men's Fraternity*. *Men's Fraternity* is a three-year program that leads men through a journey of understanding their past, defining Manhood, and helping call them to a God-sized future.

I had the opportunity to not only go through all three years, but to actually teach it to other men along the way. My soul drank up the knowledge the way flowers soak up a spring rain. I could not get enough. It helped me define Manhood. Those lessons made me understand the importance of *calling* my boys to Manhood. Those classes and being with those other men

---

[1] Confession: Every time we had a son, I said a small prayer of thanks knowing I was not going to have to pay for a wedding. Don't judge me.

changed my life, my marriage and, most importantly, helped me start to build the path I am guiding my sons down. It was then I had a true definition of my calling as "Dad."

Motivation

My genetic composition is not on my side. It is too long a story to go into, but I have some certainty when it comes to my expected lifespan. A disease called Hereditary Amyloidosis Transthyretin (hATTR) runs in my family.[2] Sure, I understand that any of us could be with Jesus by morning and not even tomorrow is guaranteed, but short of succumbing to an unexpected tragedy of some kind, if I live to 65 I will feel like I have found favor with God. (In truth, I do not have a high degree of confidence I will live to see 60.) Please do not think I take that lightly or am being flippant about it. It is something that is always on my mind. Some days I dwell on it more than others. Some days it stirs emotions in me that are too many to list. But it is something I have known for a long time. My grandfather passed away at 61. One of his brothers died at 61, too, another at 54. My uncle was 57. My father was 53. As I said, my genetic composition is not on my side.

While there is no cure for FAP, recently there have been some medical breakthroughs providing a very small measure of hope. Regardless, the impact of FAP on my life cannot be understated.

Yes, God could perform a miracle in my life. Yes, God could use modern medicine to heal me. I pray for both of those more

---

[2] If you really want to know more, check out www.amyloidosis.org/facts/familial.

often than you can imagine. But even if that happens, I do not believe the motivation I have for writing this book would change. Honestly, I am thankful for this journey, because it has certainly channeled my energy.

I know what you are thinking: "Great, Dustin. Thanks for the depressing story." But there is an important reason I shared it.

In my reality, there is a lesson for you.

Clarity and Focus

When you have clarity on any situation, it allows you to have amazing focus. You move with purpose. You become intentional more often and the "things that really matter" do not elude you. These stories are all around us.

The mother who is diagnosed with cancer who, to leave a legacy for her family, endeavors to start an orphanage in another country, and challenges her children to always think about those less fortunate.

The father whose daughter is killed by a texting driver, who turns grief into action, lobbying day and night to have texting-and-driving laws changed.

The child who, fighting for his life, speaks words of wisdom well beyond his years, gives more hope than anyone could ever give him, and teaches people about the power of friendship, community, and love.[3]

All because they were living their life with amazing clarity and focus.

---

[3] Issac Ray Steiner (01.23.06-03.06.13) you are missed, loved, and thought of often!

Hollywood recognizes the power of these stories. For example, in 1993, Michael Keaton and Nicole Kidman starred in a movie called *My Life*. Keaton plays a husband who has everything going for him. However, soon after finding out his wife is pregnant with their first child, he is diagnosed with cancer and given months to live. Knowing he will not live to see his child grow up, he begins to make a video of all the things he wants to teach his son. Everything from how to shave to how to enter a room and shake someone's hand. It is not necessarily the happiest of movies, but it tells a moving, inspirational story and is the perfect example of a man living with clarity and focus.

It certainly does not have to be (nor, ideally, will it be) something like a genetic defect or something more terrifying, like a terminal illness, that can give you the gift of clarity and focus.

Think about the soldier who knows he is leaving for his deployment. How much more valuable does his time become as his ship-out date looms? Do you think he is wasting a second doing things that have no lasting impact? What about the dad who travels for work? Doesn't he want to spend as much time with his wife and kids as he possibly can when he is home? Anytime you are faced with something that will remove you from those you love, regardless of duration or distance, you begin to cherish the precious commodity of time with them.

The problem arises when you do not have something giving you clarity and focus. You go through life on autopilot and then one day you find yourself saying, "I can't believe they are going into middle school," or, "Wow, high school already," or something scarier like, "I can't believe my boy is getting married."

When you lack clarity and focus, you look back on your life with regrets and find yourself saying, "I wish I had," "I should have," or "If I could do it over again, I would."

Now here is the good news: You can live your life right now (starting this very moment) with clarity and focus. You just have to choose to do so.

My deepest hope for you is that after reading this book, you will want to do some very specific things for your son. To accomplish that, you know what you are going to need? You guessed it: clarity and focus.

Let me give you two quick suggestions about how to choose to have more clarity and focus.

Be Passive No More

"Passive" is defined by dictionary.com as *"Accepting or allowing what happens or what others do, without active response or resistance."*

It is synonymous with words like submissive, compliant, docile, and unassertive.

Passivity is a virus that lies dormant in the soul of every man. For that virus to activate, all it needs a dash of indifference and a pinch of compliancy. Add to that the opportunity to be constantly distracted by society, technology, sports, and a hundred other things, and passivity becomes a silent killer of marriages, relationships, and the lives we were intended to live. We will talk much more about passivity in a later chapter.

Write and Share

You need to write down the things you want to accomplish. Write down your professional goals. Write down those things you want to do with your spouse and kids. Decide what matters. Decide what matters now and, more importantly, decide what will matter in 10, 25 or 50 years. Then write those things down. There is real power in putting your goals on paper in a place where you can see them regularly. There is even more power in sharing them with someone. Give your spouse, your friends, and your discipleship group permission to ask you how you are doing in reaching your goals.

Dr. Gail Matthews, a psychology professor at Dominican University of California, conducted a study on goals. She found that people who write them down, share them with a friend, and provide weekly updates to that friend are 33 percent more successful in achieving them than are people who just wrote them down.

Write down your plan. Share your plan.

My Inspiration

I mentioned how the idea for this book started with author and speaker Mark Sanborn talking about the importance of clear, concise communication. His example, and the piece that really started my mind wandering and wondering, was the Gettysburg Address.

On November 19, 1863, President Abraham Lincoln traveled to the Pennsylvania battlefield for the dedication of the National Cemetery at Gettysburg and gave one the most famous speeches in American history. But here are some things you might not know:

- President Lincoln was not the main speaker for the day. A guy you have never heard of, who served as a U.S.

Representative, a U.S. Senator, and the Secretary of State, gave the Oration that day.[4] It was two hours long and no one remembers it. By all accounts, it wasn't a bad speech, but when the President stepped up shortly after Everett for some "dedicatory remarks," history was made.

- While Everett rambled on and on, President Lincoln delivered his remarks in under two minutes.
- The Gettysburg Address has 246 words and is only 10 sentences long.

Ten sentences. It was that fact that stuck with me. I began to think about my life, my four boys, and ten sentences.

I am working to raise my boys into Godly men, but I realized that if something were to happen to me, the goals I have for them would be lost. I wanted something to leave behind for my boys to read. A message from me to them after I was gone, especially if I happen to not be here as they grow up (a la Michael Keaton in *My Life*). I wanted a letter to my boys read at my funeral. I wanted them to know what matters in this life and why. I wanted to make sure it was clear, concise, and encompassed everything I would want to share with them.

So, I set out to write them a 10-sentence letter that, for me, accomplished that.

Dear Boys,

My sons, my sons, my sons, I want you to read carefully, pay attention, and hold on to what I am about to share

---

[4] His name was Edward Everett. Ever hear of him?

with you. I want you to always honor, respect and love your mom (which means looking out for and protecting her when I am not around). Be a man of God that has Kingdom impact on your family, friends, and community by thinking differently, leading courageously, and living passionately. In case I did not have the chance to show you how to live like that, I have a group of men that will show you and they are men you can look to as Guides to follow. As you learn what it means to be a Godly man, I expect you to lead your brothers on this journey, as well as your sons, and grandsons. Even when you don't feel like it, love your wife and put her above everyone and everything by dying to self and leading as a servant because she is a Daughter of Christ. Remember you are called to honor and love her and will be held accountable to God for how well you do that. Most importantly, recognize your need for the Savior, Jesus Christ. Remember that His gift is about Grace (not about being perfect or trying to earn anything), about accepting the gift of Jesus, and then chasing him your entire life. It is the most important thing you can do. Know that I love you, am proud of you, and I always have been.

Love, Dad

Ten sentences. 258 words.

It is a letter I plan to give them as I guide them into Manhood. It is a letter that will be given to them if something happens to me before they reach that point.

As I said earlier, this is a message that is so important for them to hear. Over the course of this book, I am excited to take each of those 10 sentences and give them the depth of context and explanation needed.

It is my opportunity to pour my heart out to the four young men God has entrusted to my watch.

I invite you to read along.

Your Challenge

I have fought the good fight, I have finished the race, and I have remained faithful. And now the prize awaits me—the crown of righteousness, which the Lord, the righteous Judge, will give me on the day of His return.

2 TIMOTHY 4:7-8
THE BIBLE, NEW LIVING TRANSLATION

It matters how you are going to finish. Are you going to finish strong?

NICK VUJICIC

Finish It

Whether you have never given thought to anything like writing a letter to your son, or think you could or should, the courage you need comes in one simple idea. It can be found in the writings of the disciple Paul.

The phrase you need to hold on to, embrace, and challenge yourself to live out daily is *finish strong.* In his letter to his friend, Timothy, Paul is looking back on his life and resting in the peace of a race well run. He had followed God wherever He called, preached to everyone who would listen, fought through pain and disappointment, but was confident he ran his race to the finish. We all have a race to run and if God has entrusted you with a son, your son is major part of your race. We need to run the race to the end. We need to teach, train, guide, and help direct him to be all God has called him to be. No matter what. We need to run that race.

My letter to my boys is my way of running that race to completion, even if I may not be around to see them reach the finish line to which I am called to lead them. The problem in today's culture is that there is so much to pull us off course and stop us from running the race[1]. Tragically, we often do not even realize we have stopped running until it is too late.

Let me give you four keys to finishing strong and taking on the mindset that you will complete this race of raising your children, no matter what.

---

[1] Social media, 1,000-plus TV channels, Fantasy Football, and hundreds of other things we do wasting time.

Dump Extra Weight

We all walk around with some extra baggage. Some of us have a small fanny pack of junk while others are driving around a semi-trailer full of hurts, regrets, disappointments, and bitterness.

Please do not think I am simply saying you need to "get over" those things in your past. I am saying that you need to spend some real time evaluating where you have been, where you come from, and what things in your life have happened that make you who you are today. Maybe your father was an angry, abusive alcoholic. Instead of coming to terms with that by letting go of resentment and replacing it with God's peace, you just decide, "I have a temper because my dad did, and it's what I learned growing up. It's just who I am."

Maybe there is someone in your past who wronged you so deeply that years later you cannot even hear his or her name without emotions stirring in you. Maybe all you want is your dad, mom, old college friend, or nasty gym teacher to just come and apologize because, after what they did to you, that is the least they can do. Moreover, until they do that, you are going to allow that wound to fester as an open sore that affects every other area of your life.

Forget waiting for them. Go to God and admit that you can't carry that burden anymore. Say aloud, "Father, I forgive them because not forgiving them is ruining my life."

You can never forget your past, but without fully addressing it, examining it, and understanding the part it played in who you are today, you will never be able to fully move forward to the finish line.

The best thing I ever did for my boys was to start seeing a counselor. I was not in any kind of crisis, but meeting monthly has been a great thing. It is something I wish I'd started doing 10 years earlier; it is something I believe every person should do. Trust me, it's not a sign of weakness. It is not as scary as you think, either. It will help you address any extra psychological weight you may be carrying that is negatively affecting how you raise your son. Counselors take on many shapes and forms, but be sure to find someone who is qualified to help you explore issues in your life. This may be through a local non-profit, or even visiting with a pastor at a local church. Many churches have resources to help, or even some funds to help cover some costs of a counselor.

Learn From Others

There are two groups of people you need to have in your life to help you run your race and finish strong: mentors and accountability partners.

Mentors

A year before my dad passed away, we went Muskie fishing. It was a Christmas gift from my wife. Dad and I got to spend the day trolling for a species that can grow to over 60 inches.

We had a great time. Muskie fishing was something neither of us had ever done before. We had no idea where to start. We didn't have a boat. We didn't have the right gear. We didn't have the right bait. We didn't know how to fish for Muskie. We had never seen one in the wild.

The only things we had were $300 and a desire to catch one.

That is why we needed a guide. Mike was an expert. He spent 12+ hours a day, over 250 days a year, fishing for Muskie in Indiana or Minnesota or anywhere else he could. He had 10 different rods and four boxes of bait. He had a $25,000 boat. He had a fish finder with a screen as big as my television. It is safe to say he knew what he was doing.[2]

Here is my point: If you have a desire to *finish strong*, you need someone you can look to as a guide.

Do you have all the tools, skills, knowledge, and maps you need to achieve your goals? Do you have someone who has been there before? Someone who knows where to go, what to look for, what to say, and how to communicate it in a way you understand?

Do you have a mentor? Do you have a "wise and trusted advisor" (Webster's definition)? If not, how will you be able to *finish strong*?

Everyone needs a mentor. There are a couple of things your mentor should be and couple of things he can be.

Your mentor should be:

1. Someone you respect—You should value his opinion. You should be able to trust what he is telling you. He should be living a life you admire and want to strive for yourself.

2. Someone who has been there, done that—With four boys, it would make no sense for my mentor to only have daughters. I want someone who has been through what I am going through or will go through.

---

[2] No, we did not catch anything that day, but we still had fun. That is why it is called "fishing," not "catching!"

Your mentor can be:

1. A sounding board—The value of a mentor comes when you can sit with him and just share your heart. Share your struggles. Share your thoughts. Your plans. Your joys. Allow him to help you think through difficult situations.
2. Someone to follow—Your mentor should be someone whose life inspires you to be better. You should look at your mentor and say, "Boy, when I have teenagers, I really want that kind of relationship with my kids."

How do you get a mentor? Simple. Ask.[3]

Once you have found someone you would like to learn from, ask to meet with him. Take him to breakfast. Pick his brain. Share your heart. Simply become his friend and learn from him.

Accountability Partners

The first person to learn from is a mentor. The second is an accountability partner (or three).

> *"Two are better than one, because they have a good return for their labor. If either of them falls down, one can help the other up. But pity anyone who falls and has no one to help them up." (Ecclesiastes 4:9-10)*

---

[3] No, really. Just ask. I have found that most people are more than willing to give time and invest in someone else. They just never do because no one ever asks them.

Going through life is sort of like climbing a mountain. When climbers scale the highest mountains in the world, they make sure they stay tied to other climbers. They do this so if one slips, the others will prevent him from plummeting to a certain death.

Who are you tied to? Who can pull you back onto the trail when you slip or veer off course?

The problem is as men, most of us have lots of acquaintances or even friends, but our root system is shallow, not anchoring. We do not let anyone dig down too deep.

Do you have a small group of people you meet and talk to regularly about more than last night's ball game or the latest episode of your favorite television show? Accountability partners are your companions as you travel through life; they help make the journey safe and far more enjoyable.

Let me give you some reasons you need an accountability partner (or a small group of them):

1. **Jesus had them.** While there were 12 disciples, there were three to whom Jesus was especially close. In Mark 14, Jesus took the 12 to Gethsemane and told them to, *"sit here while I pray."* (v. 32). In the next verses, we get a glimpse of the three men Jesus leaned on. *He took Peter, James, and John along with him, and he began to be deeply distressed and troubled. "My soul is overwhelmed with sorrow to the point of death," he said to them. "Stay here and keep watch."* Jesus didn't show these heavy emotions to all 12; He shared them with the three men closest to Him.

    If Jesus needed other men to share His heart with, what makes you think you don't?

2. **You can't do it alone.** We love to wear the badge of "self-sufficiency" as if it is an honor. We take great pride in showing people what *we can do all by ourselves*. However, in every person's life, there comes a time when he needs a friend or three to lean on, like Jesus in the Garden. We need a friend to help us get through. Sometimes that means we ask for his help, insights, or opinions. There are other times that means we share our heart and ask him to pray.

   God did not create us to be alone. We see these friendships throughout the Bible. A great example is the relationship between David and Jonathan. We get a picture of how much these two men loved each other in I Samuel 18:1-4: *After David had finished speaking with Saul, Jonathan became one in spirit with David, and he loved him as himself. And Jonathan made a covenant with David because he loved him as himself. Jonathan took off the robe he was wearing and gave it to David, along with his tunic, and even his sword, his bow, and his belt.*

   David was a man chasing the heart of God, and he knew how important it was for him to have a close friend and ally.

3. **You need to hear it from a friend.** There are going to be times in your life when you will need to be told you are out of line, off course, or just plain wrong. If you are married, these may be things that would be very hard to hear from your spouse. If it relates to your role and responsibility in marriage or with your kids, your spouse may not be able to tell you. Proverbs 27:6 says, *"Wounds from a friend can be trusted."* You need someone in your life who

will speak truth to you, even when you do not want to hear it. It is never easy to hear those things, but if you have no one close enough to you who can speak that truth, you are missing out on the joys, growth, and struggles that come with *true friendship.*

I am so thankful for the few men I have in my life as my accountability partners. Men who know my heart, my struggles, and my joys. Men I can call when I have a bad day at work who encourage me to keep fighting the battle. Men I can call when my kids are causing me to lose my mind. Men who keep me focused on what matters, not what my selfish nature gravitates toward. I love them dearly and am so glad to be tethered to them as we climb. They are helping me *finish strong.*

For some helpful information on having a great accountability group, check out the *Dear Boys Extra* at the end of the chapter.

Listen to the Counselor

The third thing we need in order to finish strong is to listen to the Counselor. John 14:15 records Jesus telling us, *"If you love me, you will obey what I command. And I will ask the Father, and he will give to you another Counselor to be with you forever."*

Jesus was very clear that once we accept Him as our Savior, the Counselor (the Holy Spirit, also called an "Advocate, "Helper," or "Comforter" in some versions of the Bible) would be with us. If we will open our ears and our hearts, the Holy Spirit can be the voice that gives us everything we need to finish strong in our lives. The Holy Spirit wants to do so much for us and through us, if we are willing to submit to His power in our lives.

Here are just some of the things the Holy Spirit does

- Guides us into Truth (John 16:8)
- Leads us (Romans 8:14)
- Fills us (Ephesians 5:18)
- Produces fruit in our lives (Galatians 5:22-23)
- Transforms us into Christ's image (2 Cor. 3:18)

If we have any hope of finishing strong and completing all God has given us to do in our lives, there is no doubt that we will need the help of the third person of the Trinity: the Holy Spirit.

Focus on the Finish Line

So, to finish strong, we need to dump extra weight, learn from others, listen to the Counselor, and, finally, we need to focus on the finish line. We must always remember the race we are running and why that race is important. We cannot be so distracted with calling our sons to be great athletes, musicians, artists or students that we miss the opportunity to call them to be great men who are chasing Jesus. The Bible makes it very apparent that God wants us to raise our children in such a way that they have a clear passion to pursue Him throughout their entire lives (Malachi 2:15) and that it is our job to guide them to lives with Him (Proverbs 22:6).

If we constantly keep that in mind as the ultimate goal for our children, we will not only have amazing clarity for them, but we will be able to help them through the finish line.

A major roadblock occurs when we take our eyes off the finish line in our job as Dad. We begin to worry more about how many travel teams they are on, how many camps they go to, how many friends they have, and a thousand other things society tells us are important. We make knowing and chasing Jesus just another activity on the calendar. We not only teach them Jesus is "just another thing to do" but, worse, we model it with our own behavior and decisions.

If we want to finish strong and raise kids that have an Eternal, Kingdom-of-Christ perspective, we need to start living with an Eternal, Kingdom-of-Christ perspective in our own lives. Our sons need to see us studying our Bible more than the stats for our Fantasy Football team. They need to hear us saying "no" when we're asked to go hang with our buddies, so we can spend time with our children's mother. They need to see us praying over them at night, leading them to worship on Sunday, and keeping Christ front and center in our homes ***daily***. We cannot expect our kids to have a passion for Christ when everyone around them, including us, demonstrates no passion for Christ.

That is Some Challenge

So, with all that as your challenge, what does this book about a letter to my boys have to do with you?

My prayer is that you find encouragement and insight on your journey of fatherhood. Your challenge is to come away from this book with the confidence and guts to write a letter to your own son.

Again, nothing could be more important than to let him know exactly what he means to you, why he means so much, and how you are going to accomplish the task God gave *you* to raise *him*.

I want my letter to settle on my boys' hearts long after I am gone.

You should want that, too.

DEAR BOYS EXTRA

The Six "C's" for an Effective Accountability Group

Regardless of when they meet, how many men there are (four to six is ideal), or what the overall goals may be, there are some common things that every group needs.

Confidentiality

Everything discussed in the group has to stay in the group. No, you cannot call your wife afterwards and say, "You aren't going to believe this!" You all need to commit that when you get together, it is a safe place to share. Any concerns about confidentiality will ensure the group remains superficial and no one will open up. Lack of confidentiality is the killer of small groups.

Candor

You will only grow if you are open, honest, and vulnerable. You need to get over fear, embarrassment, or pride and be willing to share. I promise that whatever you are struggling with, you are not alone. You may just need to be the first one to speak up! Not only do you need to be candid with your own comments, you need to be candid when you speak to each other. There should be no fear of "hurting someone's feelings." However, neither do you need to be "brutally honest." We may not use that phrase, but we do say things like, "Well, I'm just going to be honest" as an excuse to tell someone the truth with no regard to their feelings. We do need be completely honest in our conversations but do we have to be brutal? Some of us love the "brutal" part too much. In fact, some of us do not know how to be honest unless we are brutal. Being honest is how we show we love and care for someone. How does being "brutally honest" accomplish that? I would argue it does not.

Consistency

You need to meet every week. Yes, schedules are tricky. I know you will travel and be gone. But, as much as possible, you need to be there! None of us has time. We make time for whatever we deem important. This is why an early morning usually works well. Unless you are out of town, you should be able to meet once a week at 5 or 5:30 a.m. The relationships are built only through proximity; you need to be close to other men and that closeness needs to happen often and consistently.

Curriculum

You need to have something you plan to discuss. It can be a chapter of the Bible. It can be a book you all want to go through together and discuss.[4] Regardless, you need to have something on your agenda. It will help give your group focus and keep your time together from turning into a gripe session about wives, kids, or work.

---

[4] Oh, I have a suggestion! Maybe a book about raising your sons?

Contact

With technology, it has never been easier to connect with people. You need to stay connected with the group. Use text messages to check in, ask for prayer for that 2 p.m. meeting, or make sure people will be at breakfast tomorrow. You cannot isolate yourself. You need to be connected. Even when the group is not meeting, you need to have regular contact with those men.

Check-Up Questions

Along with whatever you may be studying or talking about, some very honest, probing questions need to be asked every week. These questions get to the heart of issues men struggle with. They are designed to keep your life in-check, because we are prone to drift.

- How has God blessed you this week?
- How often have you read the Bible this week? Any challenges from your reading?
- How is your prayer life?
- How are you doing pursuing your wife? Have you spent intentional time with her?
- How are you doing pursuing your children? Have you spent intentional time with them?
- How are you pursuing a life of holiness? Purity with thoughts, actions, words, what you see, etc?
- Have you been 100% honest and transparent?

No, not all these questions are needed every week or perhaps even at all. Your group may have other issues or things you want to check up on. I know that last question is tricky because people can lie. But, by asking, you are going to at least make him lie to your face. And when whatever he's been lying about comes out (and it will come out), you know that you have authority to speak truth, in love, to him!

Breakfast Discussion

QUESTIONS FOR DADS:

1. What did you feel like after your son was born and you realized you had the title of "dad"?

2. What scares you most about being a dad?

3. Who were / are your mentors? What have they taught you?

4. Who are your accountability partners? Why are they important to you? *(If you do not have any, commit to your son that you will have some within two weeks.)*

QUESTIONS FOR SONS:

1. What is your earliest memory of your dad?

2. What are five words you would use to describe your dad? (Be honest! He won't be mad!)

3. What are you most excited for as you become a man?

4. What makes you nervous about becoming a man?

QUESTION FOR BOTH:

What is the one thing from this chapter that stands out to you and what will you do differently in the future?

The Letter

Sentence One

THEIR GUIDE

My sons, my sons, my sons,
I want you to read carefully,
pay attention, and hold on to what
I am about to share with you.

They are always watching

In the previous chapter, I talked about the importance of having a mentor in your life to show you the way and serve as your sounding board. Without question, as Dad, you are your son's first mentor or Guide. You are the one he looks to, to see how it is done. He watches you. He does what you do. He says what you say (for better or worse).

I remember sitting at the kitchen table one evening with my four boys and my wife. One of them spilled his milk, which seems to be a daily occurrence. This time, though, when the cup was knocked over, the clumsy child banged his fist on the table and said, "Dammit!"

He was five.

My wife looked at me. I was trying to stifle my laughter and act upset. She did not find it amusing which meant I had better not, either. Then it struck me: there was no way he had overheard or picked up that particular expression from his mother.

In that moment, my status as Guide was firmly realized.

As with most big things in our lives, we are never quite ready, but if we try to wait until we think we are, big things will never happen. We need to be constantly on guard with our words and actions because our kids soak them all up and we never know when those words or actions may be replicated by them. We can only hope it is not at a restaurant with friends or in a church while we are talking to the Pastor.

We need to embrace our role as Guide. More importantly, we have to know where we want our boys to end up, or we will have no way of knowing how to get them there. When we are ready to tell our boys something important, we want them to hear the seriousness in our voice. We want them to recognize, "What I am about to say is important. You need to pay attention. Seriously. Eyes on me." We need to live our life in such a way that they admire, love, and respect us, so when we plead for their ears, they can't help but give them to us.

My inspiration for this opening sentence came from the book of Proverbs:

- 1:8 – *Listen, my son, to your father's instruction and do not forsake your mother's teaching.*
- 2:1, 5 – *My son, if you accept my words and store my commands within you ... then you will understand the fear of the Lord and find the knowledge of God.*
- 3:1-2 – *My son, do not forget my teaching, but keep my commands in your heart, for they will prolong your life many years and bring you prosperity.*
- 4:1, 10-11, 20 – *Listen, my sons, to a father's instruction; pay attention and gain understanding. / Listen, my son, accept what I say, and the years of your life will be many. I guide you in the way of wisdom and lead you along straight paths. / My son, pay attention to what I say; listen closely to my words.*
- 5:1 – *My son, pay attention to my wisdom, listen well to my insight.*
- 6:20 – *My son, keep your father's commands and do not forsake your mother's teaching.*
- 7:1, 24 – *My son, keep my words and store up my commands within you. / Now then, my sons, listen to me; pay attention to what I say.*

Is it clear enough that we need to plead for our sons to listen? Do you have something worth saying to them? Are you living your life like a Guide, knowing they are watching and taking mental notes?

Are you living to impress your values, beliefs, and behaviors upon them?

Actually, it does not matter how you answer that question. You are. Whether you know it or not.

The best example of impressing on our children comes at the very end of the book of Proverbs and not from a dad, but a mom.

Live to Impress

The sayings of King Lemuel, an inspired utterance his mother taught him. (v1)

Proverbs 31 was written by King Lemuel. No one knows for sure who he was, and Lemuel means "for God" or "devoted to God," but Jewish tradition says King Lemuel was a poetic name for King Solomon. Whether or not that is the case (for the sake of argument, let's just go with it), that means the insight would have come from his mother, Bathsheba. Remember her story with King David?

We know the sins David and Bathsheba committed: adultery, the murder of her husband, and a cover-up. (You can read the story in 2 Samuel 11-12.) We also know the consequences of those sins: their first baby, conceived at that time, died seven days after birth. However, we also see the redemptive grace of God in their story. David was called a "man after God's own heart." If Proverbs 31 *was* written by Solomon, there is no doubt his mother had a wonderful relationship with God, too, based on Bathsheba's knowledge of the role He gave her as a helper to the King.

These 31 verses are teachings a mother wanted to impress on her son; teachings she wanted him to live by. They are a great model for us to follow. In order to impress, we need to teach. These are not sayings she simply *told* her son; she *taught* them to him. No doubt these are not things the King heard but once from his mom. She just did not hand them to him in a letter when he turned 16. She impressed them on his heart repeatedly. For that to happen, the teachings had to be in *her* heart and modeled daily.

There was constant instruction on these things. It is easy to picture her walking through the marketplace with the young Prince by her side and pointing out the prostitutes, saying, "See her and what she's doing? *That's* the kind of behavior I have been talking to you about.

He was reminded of her teachings repeatedly. Remember, these are *the sayings of King Lemuel*. His sayings, but learned from her. He embraced them as his own. See my point?

The King was saying things he was taught as a young boy by his mom. (We also see Solomon, in Proverbs, passing along his own wisdom. Wisdom he, no doubt, picked up from his mother and father.) He probably shared them with his wife. He taught them to his sons and daughters. *He* was saying them (they were in his heart and mind) long after the training and influence of his mother (and father) had ended. He probably reflected on them as part of the speech he gave at her funeral. He knew the sayings.

> *Listen, my son! Listen son of my womb! Listen, my son, the answer to my prayers! (v2-3)*

In order to impress, we need passion. In verse 2, she uses the word "listen" three times. She stresses how crucial it is that he understands these things. She realizes the consequences on his life if he does not take her words to heart. She says "listen" three times to get his attention. Each refrain invokes a stronger emotion, to truly engage her son's mind and heart.

Listen, my son! (You are my son. I am raising you, listen to me!)

Listen, son of my womb! (Not only am I raising you, but you are flesh of my flesh. I care for you as I do my own body; listen to me!)

Listen, my son, the answer to my prayers! (Not only am I raising you and caring for you like my own body, but I prayed to God for you. You were given to me by God because of a longing in my heart. God knew what He was doing when He graced me with you, so listen to me!)

The final "listen" shows God was part of her daily life and she illustrated that relationship to her children every day. They saw their mom actively engaged in a relationship with God. She was a shining example to them.

Here are two questions for you as you think about *impressing* on your sons:

1. What are you trying to teach them?

    You spend a lot of time making sure they do a lot of things (bathe, pick up toys, brush teeth, etc), but what things should you be teaching them that they will remember long after you are gone? Things like what it means to be a man of God, how to love a woman, how to treat strangers, how to control their emotions, how to memorize Scripture. Those are the things you really want them to remember. Are you not only thinking about teaching them, but *impressing* them on their hearts?

2. Are you living those teachings out yourself?

Your kids *watch your actions* much more than they *listen to you*. It does you no good to just say all the right things over and over and then:

- lose your temper and yell;
- tell them you don't have time right now to read a Bible story with them;
- blow off their question about the guy on the corner holding the cardboard sign when you have $10 in your pocket you could give him.

If you do not live out the things you want to impress on your kids, you are wasting your breath telling them how to live.

You need to *live to impress*.

Know the Destination

*"Would you tell me, please,
which way I ought to go from here?"
"That depends a good deal on where
you want to get to," said the Cat.
"I don't much care where—" said Alice.
"Then it doesn't matter which
way you go," said the Cat.
"—so long as I get SOMEWHERE,"
Alice added as an explanation.*

> *"Oh, you're sure to do that," said the Cat,*
> *"if you only walk long enough."*
> ALICE'S ADVENTURES IN WONDERLAND
> (LEWIS CARROLL, 1865)

That exchange between Alice, trying to figure out Wonderland, and the cat with the enormous grin holds deep truth for us if we view ourselves as Guides for our sons. We must have the destination clearly in mind. You must know where you want your sons to be when they reach the end of their journey with you as their Guide. Remember, we do not get to guide our boys forever, but if we "train up a child" while he is with us, if we give him a solid understanding and foundation, then "when they are old they will not depart from it." (Proverbs 22:6)

If we do not have a definite place—physically, spiritually, emotionally—to which we want to lead them, we give up Guide status and become the proverbial blind leading the blind. We spend our time trying to be their friend or letting them do whatever they assert will make them happy (or popular).

As we ponder our destination, I find there are three helpful "Guide"posts.

Know which trails matter

As Guide, you need to make sure you decide which trails are most important to spend time on. Do you spend more time on the Church Trail or the Sports Trail? Are you making the Family Trail a priority or are you easily diverted to the Always-on-the-Go Trail?

As Guide, your main destination should be to raise your boys into Godly men. If you constantly give in to them and are too busy to impress spirituality and salvation on them, you have missed the most important trail and, I believe, will be held accountable for that someday. You cannot simply lean on teachers on Sunday morning, church camps or youth groups to bring your children to a saving knowledge of Jesus. That is your primary job and you need to make sure as a family you are not running down so many other trails that you miss this one. Remember, the decision for your kids to trust in Jesus is not something we can dictate, but it is our job to direct them to a place (over and over and over) where they have the decision to make!

When weighing which trails matter, love your kid enough to say "no" to some. Remember: parent first, friend second. Yes, he may get upset, call you the worst parent ever, pout, complain that "everyone else gets to," and all those other things kids do to guilt parents into giving in. That's fine. That's why you are the parent: to make the tough decisions for the family. You laugh when your child says, "But Dad, everyone else is doing it," but, in reality, many parents use the same reasoning for never telling their kids "no." They don't want to be showed up by the cool Guides who take their kids on all the fun trails![1]

As you Guide, have a clear understanding of why you okay some trails and nix others. Never say "No, we are not going down that trail," without good reason. "Just because" or "It's too much" won't cut it. You have to be able to explain your rationale. It is absolutely fine to tell your son, "We are too busy for you to do that, so you can't." However, use those moments to

---

[1] If one of my boys doesn't call me "the worst father ever" at least once a month I take it as a sign I am not doing my job!

talk to him about the importance of time management, the cost of things, and the value of family time rather than always having to be somewhere or do something.

Be ready to talk to him about the lasting value of some trails versus the fleeting value of others.

Know the best trail for him

Believe in your son's abilities and desires and help foster those things. Each child is unique so each has different things he will excel at and like to do. Make sure you recognize those things in him and help develop those skills. Look for trails that set him up for challenge and opportunities for success. Do not always look for the toughest trail or the one he definitely does not want to walk, even if you are guiding.

Do not make your son take the Football Trail if he would rather take the Theater Trail. Remember, your trails (athletics, academics, or vocations) may be very different from his. That is okay, because God may not have created him to follow in your path. As Guide, you need to make sure your son gets to where *he* is supposed to go, even if you would rather he end up somewhere else.

As it says in 1 Corinthians 10:23, everything may be permissible, but not everything is beneficial. Just because it is a trail open to your son does not mean he needs to journey down it. Help him find the trails he really likes to walk and encourage him to follow you. Steer him to those trails that promote lifelong skills you can help him build on.

Know when to let him be out front

My oldest son and I recently spent some time in the woods with another father and son. The other dad and I loved walking well behind our sons. We watched as they talked, laughed, and led the way. It was a great reminder that sometimes we need to let our sons be out front.

This is a very hard principle for a Guide to understand. The joy in walking the trail is the view, especially from the front. It has been said that only the lead dog's view changes. The rest of the sled dogs stare at ... well, you know what they stare at!

As Guide, you need to let your son be out front, with you behind him, making sure he keeps to the trail. He will relish the view and be excited about what is next—and that is great because, at some point, he will be on the trail alone. He needs the practice of being out front with the safety and security of you behind him.

When he is out front, it does not make your job as Guide any easier. In fact, it may be harder than when he is following.

Remember a few important things when he is up ahead:

- No matter what, he must walk the trail. You cannot drag or force him along. You need to give guidance and instruction on how best to walk it, but you cannot do it for him.

- He is going to be so distracted looking all around that you need to be looking ahead. If you are not paying attention to where the trail will take him, he could slip, walk into something, or end up somewhere he ought not be. You need to be vigilant and teach him the importance of focus and attention.[2]

- He will have all the confidence he needs when he knows you are behind him. The encouragement of your voice and your strong hand steadying him will communicate he can do it!

Being a Guide to my four sons is such an important part of my life. It is an important part of your life, too, I know. I hope you wake up every day and give thought to, pray about, and seek wise counsel from mentors and friends about where you are guiding your son.

Remember, he is watching you.

---

[2] If you have ever helped your son learn to drive, you know this! I already break out in a cold sweat when I think about my boys behind the wheel of a car, me in the passenger seat, slamming the imaginary brake and holding on for dear life.

Breakfast Discussion

QUESTIONS FOR DADS:

1. Can you think of a time when your son copied something you did that you wish he hadn't? Or something he learned from you that he still does (good or bad)?

2. If you could impress one thing on your son, what would it be? Only one. Use fewer than three sentences.

3. Which trails did your dad lead you on or allow you to go down when you were growing up? Did he ever force you down any trails?

QUESTIONS FOR SONS:

1. What is something your dad does that you know you should imitate?

2. What is something your dad does you think he probably shouldn't do or you never should do?

QUESTION FOR BOTH:

What is the one thing from this chapter that stands out to you and what will you do differently in the future?

Sentence Two

YOUR MOM

I want you to always honor, respect, and love your mom (which means looking out for and protecting her when I am not around).

Their First Love

If you want to ensure, as best you can, that your son has a great marriage when he is grown, there is one thing you must do: Love your wife.

Your wife will be your son's first love. He will be drawn to her in the special way babies are to the women who carry and provide for them. A newborn will hear his mother's voice and stop crying (or start). He will *smell* her and know she is near. This bonding deepens as he grows.

Mom is the first one a child runs to when he is hurt. When he is sick, he looks to her for healing, care, and a loving touch. Little boys say things like, "Mommy, when I grow up, I want to marry you!" The relationship between mother and son is God-designed and no doubt a special one.[1]

Every morning (and I mean *every*), from the time he could talk and walk until he was about five, my youngest son would run down the hallway toward our bedroom. "Princess," he would call out as he ran to my wife to give her a hug, kiss, and cuddle. She would open her arms and say, "Good morning, my prince!" To him, she was his world, as every mom should be to her toddler.

This is where my role begins. His mom is his Princess and he knows the Princess is married to me. He also knows that a Princess is to be protected, cared for, and loved.[2] So, as soon as he sees me *not* protecting, caring for, and loving the Princess, I have introduced him to something he cannot comprehend. He

---

[1] At times, this bond can go too far, last too long, and ultimately **hurt** the son. For now, we will just focus on all the good comes from that relationship.
[2] Thank you, Mr. Disney.

has to decide what to do with that: *Why would he treat a Princess that way? Is that how Princesses are really to be treated?*

See, the relationship you have with your wife is on full display and your son is watching. You may be able to go to dinner with friends and put on a happy face. You may yell all the way to church then step out of the car acting like the happiest family there. However, you cannot hide that—or anything—from your boys at home. Please do not fool yourself by saying things like, "Oh, we never fight in front of the kids," or "That stuff isn't hurting anyone," or the worst one, "The kids will be better off if we just divorce."

Lies. Bald-faced lies.

If you do not believe me, find an adult who had parents with issues they thought they were hiding or who divorced. Ask that person this one question: *Would you want your child's memories of family life to be better than yours?*

In his answer, and in his eyes, you will see the reality beneath the lies that destroy families every day.

The answer will be a resounding "YES!" Any adult who lived through parents who fought, had addictions, were in debt—or even who simply did not *show* love to each other—will tell you he wishes a better childhood for his child. Some of those adults struggle with relationships 10, 20, 30 years later, because what they witnessed growing up is seared into their souls.

Remember my advice in an earlier chapter to see a counselor to dump extra weight? That extra weight is almost always "family issues." That is why it is so important that I model how to love the Princess. The relationship I have with my sons' mom is the foundation they will come back to in *every* relationship they are ever in with a woman (friends, dating, engagement, and marriage).

It absolutely sets the direction for how well they will love their wife *and* how their relationship with their mom will evolve.

That brings me to another relationship you are modeling and need to remember: the relationship between you and your mom, your child's grandmother.

It will be easiest for boys to notice your relationship with your wife because they see it every day. They will, no doubt, learn how to treat women by watching that. But as they get older, they will begin to watch how you treat *all* women … and mirror that. So, the relationship you have with your mom is critical, too. Here's why:

You are modeling for them how to live in between two very important women in your life (and someday in theirs): mother and wife. If you do not model living well between those two women, it is a quick spiral down to conflict, hurt feelings, and broken relationships.

If the relationship with Mom is not healthy, and if there is not a healthy break as the boy becomes a man, all of the emotional baggage from his relationship with his mom is carried directly into his relationship with his wife.

A man who has not had a clean, healthy break from his mom simply looks for another woman into whom he can plug his emotional umbilical cord.

While I model how my boys should treat their mom by how I love her, I also model through the relationship they see me have with my own mom. We are going to talk about how our sons are to love their wives in another chapter, but remember this: How your son will love his wife starts with how you love his mother and grandmother.

Obviously, we have to know what it means to truly love our

wife, so they can see it. I want to start with my foundational verse as a husband. 1 Peter 3:7:

> *In the same way, you husbands must give honor to your wives. Treat your wife with understanding as you live together. She may be weaker than you are, but she is your equal partner in God's gift of new life. Treat her as you should so your prayers will not be hindered.*

In a later chapter, I am going to take this same verse and apply it to our boys' wives, but here I want to apply it in the context of their relationship with their mom. There are three key ideas I use in my letter and they are found inside that verse and others: *honor, respect, love.*

They are the things I have to keep in mind *daily* if I am going to model what loving a Princess looks like to my little princes. If I do these things well, they will grow into the men God is calling them to be, and will have a relationship with their mom that will be a blessing for their entire lives.

Honor Her

Think of the most famous woman in the world you would like to meet. Anyone at all, living or dead. Who would it be?

Mother Teresa? Princess Diana? Princess Kate? Lady Gaga?[3]

Have her in mind? Good. Now imagine you are at a small dinner party and she walks into the room. Better yet, she is going to be sitting right beside you for dinner! Can you see it in your

---

[3] No judgment here, I promise!

mind's eye? Imagine how the dinner and evening unfold. Think about the conversations you would have with her. There is so much you are curious about; so much you want to discuss with her.

Did you just notice that little twinge in your gut? Did your heart start to beat faster? Those are physical responses to your mind telling you that you are in the presence of someone you want to honor.

Back to the dinner party: Picture how you would behave around her. Envision how you would engage her in dialogue. Would you interrupt her? Would you try to "outdo" her stories? Would you expect her to get up and serve you?

Of course not! There is no way you would, because *that is not what honor looks like.*

Question: Is that how you act when you are at a dinner party with your wife?

Ouch.

Question: Is that how you act when you are at home with your wife?

Double Ouch.

In case you are still feeling too good about yourself: Is that how you treat your mom when she comes over for dinner?

Point made?

But honestly, isn't that how we would want our sons to always treat their mom? No matter the age. No matter the marital status. We want them to always give her honor.

Here are some of the words used to define "honor": *high respect, fame, glory, high public esteem.*

Honor is looking at a person and thinking, "Wow." It is holding that person in such regard that when it comes to conflicting wants, you yield. When a decision needs to be made, you always look to meet the other's desires.

We are going to talk about respect next, but do not confuse honor and respect. Respect is something a person earns because of position, title, or actions. You can respect someone without honoring them. You show respect by not offending and not challenging.

Respect is yielding because you *have* to; honor is yielding because you *want* to.

Respect is earned.

Honor is granted.

There is one more point about honor I want to make and it is an important one. It is something that your boys need to understand, especially as they get older, move out, get married, and become men. It is a point that some men, regardless of age, have never come to terms with, and because they haven't, they find themselves having to choose to side with their wife or their mother.

Honor does not mean Obey

When I was a child, I talked like I child, I thought like a child, I reasoned like a child. When I became a man, I put childish ways behind me. (1 Corinthians 13:11).

Ephesians 6:1 and Colossians 3:20 make it clear that children are called to obey their parents. Paul makes every effort to point out that home life goes best when there is order and the parents are in charge. But, as one of the Ten Commandments in Exodus 20:12 reminds us, we are called to *"Honor your father and mother."*

Through Holy Spirit-inspired words, the writers of these well-known verses chose to use very different words.

Children *obey* their parents.

Grown men *honor* their parents.

As our sons grow, we need to make sure they never lose honor for their mom. But they are not to obey her (or their dad, for that matter) forever. They need to be freed from the guilt a child feels when he disobeys. They need to be freed from the shame and disappointment cast upon them by us when they do not obey.

When a boy grows up, if the control of or need to obey his mom is not broken, you have a man who cannot stand up for himself, his wife, or his family. A wife who has ever thought or said, "I am not your mother," to her husband is married to a man who never had a clean and healthy break from his mom. If, as dads, we do all things necessary to guide and call our boys, and we do them well, this break will happen and it will happen in a way that is healthy and beneficial for everyone.

We need to make sure our boys always honor their mom. They need to see us always granting her honor, not just in public, but in the everyday moments at home. We need to be modeling honor. But, that is just the first of three very important themes we need to teach our boys about their mom.

Respect Her

I spank my children.

Please do not send me affronted emails, links to articles about why I should not, or tell me that I am causing irreversible damage to my sons' psyches. I have a Biblical responsibility to teach and raise my boys. I do not have the luxury to "spare the rod." I will answer to God as to how well I raise them and, as a loving father, I will use many different means to do that. That said, please do not think I beat my children or even spank them regularly for every little act of disobedience. That is far from the truth. In fact, I am very slow to spank. And once they reach seven or eight, spanking does not work to correct behavior, but rather gets compliance out of fear and will ultimately breed anger and resentment in them.

If you need a simple test to see if you are spanking for the right reasons, remember this: discipline is something you do for the good of the child. Punishment is something you do to make yourself feel better.

Never spank in anger.

Never.

As I said, I am very slow to spank. But there are some non-negotiables in our home. Under the age of seven, if my boys break one of these rules, he will be spanked. We don't discuss it. I don't wait while he tells me his side of the story. There is no "Let me think about what I should do." I know what to do. Get the paddle.[4]

My rules for an automatic spanking:

1. Tell a lie.
2. Disrespect your mother.

I mentioned that respect is something very different than honor. Respect is something that a person earns and is given because of their title or status. You may not like the President. You may not choose to honor him. But he is due a certain level

---

[4] Yes, I have a paddle. I don't want to use a belt or my hand. The paddle is only used for discipline.

of respect because of his title and position. You may not agree with the official's call during the game. You many not choose to show him honor. But you need to show him some level of respect because of his position.

Here is why disrespecting their mother results in automatic discipline. Before she is the boys' mother, she is ***my wife.*** I do not care who you are, disrespect my wife and I have a problem. If you are my six-year-old son and disrespect my wife, I am going to do something about it. If you are my 13-year-old son and disrespect my wife, I am going to do something about it. If you are my 35-year-old son and disrespect my wife, I am going to do something about it.

I will always defend her. Always.

As we raise our boys, we need to strive to show them their mom is worthy of their respect not only because of her title, but because she has their best interest in her heart. Once they know that and truly believe it, they will be more willing to respect her. They will listen to her counsel. They will seek her guidance.

As with honor, our boys need to witness us modeling that respect with their mom and all women. As soon as a man thinks he does not have to respect a woman, he begins a downward slide that leads to abuse of power and often verbal, emotional, or physical abuse. A son needs to see us showing respect to every woman with whom we come in contact. He needs to see us holding open doors and pulling chairs out for women. If we do not model it, what right do we have to expect him to do it?

Our boys need to honor their mom. Our boys need to respect their mom. There is one more theme we need to teach our boys in relating to their mom.

Love Her

Like honor and respect, our boys should love their mom for their entire life. Like honor, love is a choice; it is something we choose to show. Love looks like honor because it says "you are greater than me," and "I want to give all of me to help you be all you can be." But it is different in that love will involve some tough conversations. Love will look out for someone's best interest and well-being, even if the person being loved is hurting himself or herself. Love will protect not merely from others, but from self.

I want my boys to always love their mom. After I am gone, if their mom were to do things to herself that our sons saw as harmful or hurtful, I want them to know they need to say something. Even if she does not want to hear it and may not listen, they need to speak up. In the moments of those tough conversations, love will not feel like honor or respect. In those moments, they are loving her in a way I would if I were still alive.

I want to give my boys permission to step into a part of their mom's life where honor and respect may not necessarily allow them to go. There may come a time when they need to take care of her and make difficult decisions. I want them to do that in love. I want the love for their mom be the foundation on which their honor and respect is built.

While my boys are young and cannot fully understand this, nor be expected to act upon it, as they get into their teen years, I absolutely want them paying attention to what is going on with people around them, people they love. If they see someone they love in trouble, I want them to speak up. A friend at school, another brother, their mom, me. It doesn't matter. If they are worried about someone they care about, I want them to know it is crucial and commendable to step up and say something!

I know I sound like a broken record here but, as with honor and respect, our boys need to see us model the kind of love we are asking them to have. They need to be protecting and caring for their mom. They need to see us *always* having her best in mind. Ask yourself: Am I loving her in a way I want them to love her when I am gone?

Honor. Respect. Love.

All are things we need to teach our boys to give their mom. All are things we need to model with their mom. All will lead to a rich and positive relationship with their mom, no matter their age or hers.

Breakfast Discussion

QUESTIONS FOR DADS:

1. What is one thing you do to honor your wife?

2. What is one thing you do to respect your wife?

3. What is one thing you do to love your wife?

QUESTIONS FOR SONS:

1. Have you seen your dad honor, respect, and love your mom recently? What did he do?

2. How do you show your mom honor, respect, and love?

QUESTION FOR BOTH:

What is the one thing from this chapter that stands out to you and what will you do differently in the future?

Sentence Three

YOUR MANHOOD

Be a man of God that has a Kingdom impact on your family, friends, and community by thinking differently, leading courageously, and living passionately.

The Death of a Boy

Defining Manhood. There might not be a more important chapter in this whole book. It almost could have been broken up into three separate chapters, but I've kept it to one, with several different sections.[1]

I have created and proclaimed a definition of Manhood as my own. Without it, my letter would simply become a very nice letter written by a father to his sons. Without it, the letter would be well-intentioned but intention-less. A father who is simply "there" for his boys, or is even somewhat "engaged," could write this letter and not include this sentence.

If I am the Guide, this sentence is the North Star. It is what my boys point to when they need to answer the question, "What does it mean to be a man?"

If you were to ask 10 men that question, you would very likely get 10 different answers. Most are not really sure, though, and just hope they are doing all the things Manhood requires of them. 1 Corinthians 16:13 (NASB) says:

> *Be on alert, stand firm in the faith,*
> *act like men, be strong.*

"Act like men." The apostle Paul is clearly calling us to something. But what?

I want to *call* my boys to Manhood. Without a call, they will not get there. They will wander hopelessly, muddling through until they have an identity crisis because they are not sure if

---

[1] That's why it's the longest chapter in the book. Take your time reading this one! Read it twice!

Sentence Three **YOUR MANHOOD**

they are men, or perhaps even who they are at all! Without a call to something greater (Manhood, as God intended), boys will grow up physically, men on the outside but boys on the inside.

Matt Chandler, Pastor of The Village Church in the Dallas, Texas area, calls these boys trapped in men's bodies "guys." Guys are nothing more than boys who can shave.

In his book *The Myth of Adolescence*, Dr. David Allen Black explores the idea of *adolescence* and how, culturally, it is a relatively new concept. It has become a word we use to excuse behavior, especially in men. We allow them to carry their boy-like behavior into their late teens, twenties, and beyond. It is the reason guys aged 18 to 34 are among the most targeted demographics for advertisers. Guys have jobs (and money), but no sense of responsibility. They spend as much time playing video games every week as 12 to 17 year-olds, according to Statista.com. They are the reason movies like *Jackass, Hall Pass, The Hangover* and so on are box-office smashes. Those films speak directly to a group of guys who should be men based on age and responsibility, but who still act like juveniles.

Have you ever said, "Boys will be boys"? That is fine if the boys you are talking about really *are* boys. It is anything but fine if you are talking about a group of 34 year-olds who are married with kids! Almost immediately after Paul gives us a Biblical passage about love that is read at countless weddings (I Corinthians 13:4-8), he gives us this in verses 11-12:

> *When I was a child, I spoke like a child,*
> *I thought like a child, I reasoned like a child.*
> *When I became a man, I gave up childish ways.*

Notice there is no transitional period between childish behavior and Manhood. It does not say, "After finding myself for a few years, when I became a man …." No. You were a child. Then you became a man.

But that transition does not happen without a calling from and an affirmation by dad. If dad does not give those to a son, he will grow up to be a "guy," a far cry from being a "man."

Our society is populated by boys in men's bodies. Unfortunately, guys are not mature enough for marriage, so divorce rates skyrocket, pornography is pervasive, one in four women are victims of physical, sexual, or emotional abuse, and society degenerates. As a dad, I have to help my boys on their journey to Manhood. I need to help them transition from boy to man. The little boy who doesn't want to grow up, deal with adult issues, and face the challenges in front of him as a man, a husband and a father … that boy must die. I must call him to something greater!

Still, we cannot call our boys away from boyhood without calling them to something different. If we do not have anything we are calling them to, we are damning them to the "land of guys" forever.

I once heard Pastor and author Judah Smith say, "A father doesn't say, 'Go that way.' He says, 'Follow me.'"

I need to do more than just *call* my boys to Manhood. I need to do more than point the way.

I need to be *walking* the Manhood path and *living* it out in my own life. If I am not, calling to my sons is nothing more than a hollow promise that they'll enjoy someplace I've never been.

I firmly believe that most fathers who have sons do not do this well because the fathers have no idea where they are going in their own journey. The last thing those "guys" should do is call their sons on a pointless journey, to a destination they are not sure even exists.

Maybe that describes you. Maybe you do not know where to walk, so you are afraid to ask your boys to follow. If so, use my definition of Manhood. Please start with this path. Use these points. Adapt them. Change them. Use them as a foundation and build a destination and definition of Manhood that you believe in and can call your boys to join you.

You have to embrace a path, look at the boys behind you, and confidently call, "Follow me."

Manhood, This Way

This is my path. I have claimed this statement for myself and my boys as my calling to Manhood. This is where I want my life to point to and what I walk towards as I ask my boys to join me. I strive daily to apply these principles and actions to my life.

They are what I walk toward, and what I want my boys to walk toward every day of their lives, even after I am gone. I truly believe if I lead my boys in this direction, there will be blessings for them, for my wife, for my future daughters-in-law, grandkids, great-grandkids, and beyond. These tenets and my effort to impress them on my sons will be my legacy. It is how I am defining Manhood and it is my personal mission statement.

A Word About Ceremonies

I want to talk about the importance of ceremonies and using them as we call our sons to Manhood. In his book *Raising a*

Modern-Day Knight, Robert Lewis walks through the ceremonies he led his boys through on their journey to Manhood. You can use his or create your own. The critical thing to remember is this: There need to be ceremonies as reminders.

In Native American cultures, there was a very clear moment a man could point to and say, "That's when I became a man." He went into the wilderness. Maybe he made his first animal kill. Maybe he had a vision. Whatever it was, when he came back, he no longer hung around the women. He was with the men. He went on the hunting parties. He went off to war. He was a man.

There is power in ceremony. It is why we have them for graduations, weddings, deaths, and any other major life event we want to commemorate. It only makes sense to have the same kind of ceremonies as we lead our boys to Manhood. They do not have to be elaborate. They can be simple things that will allow you, as Dad, to point back to them with your son and say, "Remember when ..." I do not know what all the ceremonies I will have with my boys will look like, or even if they will look the same for all four boys, but I do know I plan to have four for each. One when they turn 13. One when they turn 16. One when they graduate high school. One when they get married.

A couple of years ago, I was honored to attend a Manhood ceremony. The son was turning 13. What a great night! Dad invited eight men to a cabin to enjoy dinner with his son. Included in the group were his son's two grandfathers and his great-grandfather. The dad gave each guest a topic to talk to his son about. He provided no real direction; he just said, "Dustin, I want you to talk about leadership. Keep it under five minutes."

I am not sure I can describe the feelings I had, sitting there.

I had the urge to *remove my sandals* because I felt like I was on holy ground.

I was rapt listening to the two grandfathers speak about work ethic and patience, and the great-grandfather speak about integrity. I was moved to tears of joy thinking about the days ahead when I can provide and share those moments with my boys. I was further moved to tears because as I watched these two older generations speak wisdom and truth to their grandson, I missed my grandfather and my dad. In fact, I missed them more in that moment than any other in recent memory. Proverbs 20:7 says, *"The righteous who walks in his integrity—blessed are his children after him!"*

I saw that verse live and breathe in the company of those four generations that night.

Earlier in the evening, my friend's wife asked if I had any thoughts or tips for making it a successful. I looked at her, smiled, and said, "The fact your husband took the time to plan this night puts him ahead of 98 percent of the fathers out there."

The power of the ceremony lies in the effort.

The ceremony only happens with effort.

After all of us spoke, the dad talked about our different subjects as being foundational to Manhood. Then he introduced his son to the four characteristics of Authentic Manhood he had learned and wanted to call his son to: reject passivity, accept responsibility, lead courageously, and expect God's greater reward. He encouraged his son to come along on this journey to Manhood. He challenged his son to hold **him** accountable to being an authentic man the son would want to follow. He told his son the men in this room were men he relied on and were men his son could rely on, too. He wrapped up the ceremony with these words: "I want every man here to know how much I love you. How proud I am of you. How great a son you are."

I cried again.

Five years later, I attended the ceremony for his second son and it was even more powerful. This time, we as a group of men were joined by the 18-year-old brother sharing his perspectives.

So as you come to a definition of Manhood you plan to chase after and call your sons toward, remember to plan some ceremonies along the way.

Now, on to my definition.

My Definition of Manhood

Be a man of God that has a Kingdom impact on my family, friends, and community by thinking differently, leading courageously, and living passionately.

This is not just my definition of Manhood; it is my personal mission statement. I want to dissect this definition into four key parts: Kingdom impact, thinking differently, leading courageously, and living passionately.

Kingdom Impact

Near the end of his life, the Apostle Paul wrote to Timothy, whom he loved like a son. In 2 Timothy 4, Paul tells Timothy, *"I have fought the good fight, I have finished the race, and I have remained faithful."*

What exactly were Paul's fight and race? To do that which God called him to. As a follower of Jesus, we have a very clear race to run. We are to love people and share what He did for them on the cross. I sum all this up in two words: Kingdom impact.

In everything I do, I want to make sure I am having an impact for the Kingdom of Jesus. I should find a career I enjoy and am good at. I do not necessarily believe we are always "called by God" to a certain job. He created us. He has designed us with gifts and abilities. We were given spiritual gifts when we surrendered to Jesus (1 Corinthians 12:8-10). I believe He wants us to use those gifts and abilities. Use them in your home and whatever job you choose to have. But use them to point people to Jesus! Regardless of where I am or what I am doing, I need to make sure I can have a positive impact for Jesus.

In the first chapter, I talked about "clarity and focus." It is that same clarity and focus I have as I think about Kingdom impact. If what I am doing in all areas of my life is not pointing people to the love, grace, and forgiveness of Jesus Christ, I need to question why I am doing it. Sure, life happens and goes on; every day cannot be a mission trip to a developing country. For example, as I am writing this sentence on a Saturday morning in February, I am sitting in the bleachers of a swimming complex. I am watching my two middle sons warm up and get ready for a swim meet. We will be here until after lunch. So, on a morning like this, how do I have Kingdom impact?

I pay attention to my actions. I give thought to my words. As I see people and talk with other parents, is my speech uplifting and encouraging? Am I looking for opportunities to connect with someone I do not know? Jesus said, "Your love for one another will prove to the world that you are my disciples." (John 13:35)

Love. I have Kingdom impact when I love. Everyone. The mark of true Christians is the way they love people. For me, the mark of a true man of God is how I love.

As I call my boys to Manhood, I need to call them to something greater than themselves. They need to have Eternal filter and focus. I want them to become men who have a real and lasting impact for the Kingdom of Jesus with the people with whom they interact. This starts at home (family), includes the people they spend time with (friends), and extends to having a heart for the part of the world God placed them in (community).

Thinking Differently

Unless you think differently, nothing will change. Unless you think differently, your kids, marriage, job, budget, life will turn out just like everyone else's. Now be honest. Have you ever said, "I hope my kids turn out just like everyone else's"? Has anyone?

I want my boys to have a different perspective. I want them to challenge the status quo. I want them to look at what is going on around them and how the rest of the world handles it, then challenge themselves to think about it differently.

The area where I most want them to have a different perspective (especially from guys) is how they think about being passive. I have been on this journey toward being a man for a long time. I have talked to dozens and dozens of guys struggling in their lives. There is one core thing that keeps showing up. There is one issue that will impact the way my boys will think more than any other.

It is something I had to recognize, call out, and deal with in my own life before I ever saw real change: passivity.

The Silent Killer

C.S. Lewis held that pride is the root of all sin. In other words, every sin out there, at its core, comes back to pride.

I firmly believe that about passivity. Passivity in men is the root issue from which nearly every other issue, struggle, demon, or vice arises. It is why we need to "think differently" than the rest of the guys around us.

When I speak to women about men's issues, one of their most common complaints is the predicament of having a passive husband. He may well be loving, caring, and a good provider. She may even say he is "engaged" in the family life, but he is just passive.

This is the husband who isn't *leading* his family. He is content to let his wife to do his job and it is wearing on her and on their marriage. Ironically, most women see their husband's passivity as a positive when they are dating or first married. It looks like "sensitivity," right?

"Oh, he always lets me pick what we do!"

"He is so sweet, he gives me whatever I want!"

The problem is that after being a married for a while, they look to him to stand up, step up, and lead. Sadly, he is too passive and remains more than happy to let her lead.

Passivity is something that almost every man deals with.

Passivity is something that can ruin a marriage.

Passivity is something that can drive kids away from their dad.

If you do not think passivity is a problem, look at how many guys with real jobs and responsibilities spend more time in a week playing video games, drinking with buddies, and stressing over their Fantasy Football team than they do playing an active role in their homes. Who do you think is forced to lead those homes while the guys are out playing?

It is far from easy to overcome passivity. It is the area in my life where I have struggled the most. It has caused more strife in my marriage than I care to talk about. It is the one thing that could keep me from leading my boys to Manhood if I don't constantly keep it in check.

Passivity was Adam's sin way back in the Garden of Eden. Adam's passivity was what the snake went after when he approached Eve with the fruit. According to Genesis 3:6, Adam was right there and saw the whole thing go down. Adam was a coward. He knew the fruit was off limits. In fact, God gave Adam the rules and Adam had in turn supposedly given them to Eve because she knew the fruit was off limits. When God came calling a couple of verses later, He asked Adam what happened and, like the coward Adam was, he looked at God and said (imagine saying this to God), *"The woman whom you gave me to be with, she gave me the fruit of the tree and I ate."* (Genesis 3:12)

Did you see what Adam did? He **blamed God and Eve**! He took no ownership or responsibility for his lack of action. Ever since then, men have been dealing with this passivity. Adam wasn't just missing a rib; he was missing a backbone.

Passivity is what will cause you to wake up one day and realize your son is 13 but you have not talked with him about sex or pornography, which you should have done years earlier (more on that later). Or you wake up and he is pulling out of the driveway with his car packed for college and you have that sinking feeling you have not prepared him.

Passivity is what keeps you from killing the boy inside you, facing your issues, and chasing after Manhood for yourself. Passivity is what is keeping you from leading your wife the way she has been praying for since before you were married. Passivity is what has allowed your kids to drift away from you without you noticing. Passivity is what keeps you from chasing a dream. Passivity is what keeps you from leading your family in prayer at the dinner table. Passivity is what keeps you staying home from church as your wife asks you to go yet again. Passivity keeps you from listening to the message and connecting with others when you do go to church.

Passivity is what, in my definition of Manhood, my boys need to "think differently" about. I need to constantly remind myself to think differently and curb my natural tendencies to behave like every other guy. I need to reject passivity and call on my boys to reject it as well. I want them to be all God created them to be and they never will get there if they do not think differently than much of the rest of the world.

My boys have to see me reject passivity and I need to help them recognize it and overcome it in their own lives.

Beating Passivity

There is no sure-fire "how to beat passivity" list anywhere, but let me give you two things that I have found help.

1. Recognize it – You have to be able to recognize where passivity has crept into your life. You have to start to look for areas where you are timid, stand-offish, or hesitant to engage. Start in your own home. In your marriage. If you do not see it, ask your wife where you need to step up

more. Did you feel that little twinge inside you when I said *ask your wife*? That is passivity raising its head. Recognize that twinge. Whenever you feel it, fight back!

2. Replace the role model – Adam's passivity lives in every man. If we want to keep it from rising up, we need to replace it. Jesus is the model. He is the last Adam and we can have Him live His life through us. When we trust Jesus as our Savior, we recognize that His way is better. His life is greater than ours. His abilities are superior to ours. When we submit to His authority, the Holy Spirit empowers us to live lives we could never live on our own. We need Jesus' power as the antidote to Adam's passivity.

As I look at my boys and say, "Follow me. I'll show you what it means to be a man of God," at the top of my list is thinking differently than the passive guys around them.

It's On You

Have you ever said to your son, "You need to take responsibility for your actions"? Good if so, because you will have no ability to argue this section with me.

As husbands and fathers, to think differently, we need to do more than reject our natural passivity. We need to accept the responsibility we have for our family.

We need to accept the responsibility we have to God in answering for how well we loved, led, and protected our wife and kids. Maybe you love Ephesians 5:23 that says you are the "head of the wife." That's fine, but before you go throwing that title of "head" around, you better know what it means.

Covenant Head

Men, we are the covenant head of the home in the same way Jesus is the covenant head of the Church. We need to remember that marriage is a covenant, not a contract.

Men are used to contracts. We are used to negotiations at work. We follow our favorite teams and players and their contracts. We study our cell phone contracts. But marriage is not a contract, which is a really good thing, because a contract says, "I want to get as much as I can without having to give up any more than I have to."

Re-read that sentence: "I want to get as much as I can without having to give up any more than I have to." Does that sound like a good approach to marriage or raising boys? No way!

A covenant says I will give all I can to you, protect you, and be accountable for everything that happens. When we marry, we are entering a covenant and men become the covenant head. In doing so, we are saying that we will take responsibility for all that happens under our watch. This is why God called to Adam in Genesis after they ate the apple. Adam, not Eve, needed to answer for what had happened.

Just like Jesus. Jesus is the covenant head of the Church. While man has sinned and is separated from God, Jesus has taken responsibility—and the punishment—for our sins. This is why He died on the cross. For us. Instead of us.

Using Jesus as our model, in the same way, we need to be the covenant head of our marriage and family. That does not mean we rule with an iron fist (more on leading courageously soon); it means that we need to be fully on guard with all that is happening in our family, because we will be held accountable.

Here are some questions to think about as the covenant head of your house:

- Do you know what television shows your wife watches?
- Do you know what movies your kids watch?
- Do you know what books they read?
- Do you know what other influences you are allowing in their lives?

I am not saying this means you tell your wife to stop watching that show or put down that book—unless you feel that show or book is detrimental to her walk with Jesus, then you *absolutely* need to say something. You need to do so, though, in a loving way, challenging her and letting her decide.

If your kids are listening to questionable music, watching sketchy YouTube videos, or reading books that open their minds to harmful ideas, as Dad, you better say something!

I am fully convinced that as men, we will answer for the things we allowed in our homes that influenced our wife and kids. I need to be willing to accept responsibility for that. When I decided to accept responsibility, it put into motion something very important:

My vigilance.

See, if I know I am responsible, I will be much more engaged. I will want to have a say. I will want to be kept in the loop about what is going on. I will have an opinion. Deciding to accept responsibility for my family is the catalyst to make sure I reject passivity and lead courageously. As men, we were created for this. We cannot ignore it or defer it. We need to step up and accept our overarching responsibility head on!

A sure litmus test to see if you are thinking differently is how well you reject passivity and accept responsibility.

Lead Courageously

Once my boys understand how to think differently, they need to embrace courageous leadership.

We need to be men who lead our families with courage. A family needs a leader. It needs someone who is in the vanguard, guiding them in the right direction. It needs someone to look to when things are not going well. When storms come. When difficulties abound. When tragedy strikes. When things are, or feel like they are, crumbling.

There needs to be a strong voice saying, "I am here. Follow me."

A family without a strong leading presence will, no matter how stable, always feel somewhat adrift. Something will not be quite right. It may be working, but it is not becoming all it can be.

A family needs a courageous leader. Boys need a courageous leader. They need a courageous leader to follow.

Follow the Leader

As men, we need to make sure we know what it means to lead our family. We need to know we are on the right path and then, with confidence, look at our wife by our side, our kids behind us, and say "Follow me." As men, we have many different places we can look to, to know what it means to be the leader.

We can look to present culture. We are inundated with images of what "men" are like. Unfortunately, whether you examine television shows, movies, social media, or media outlets, you will be hard pressed to find a model worth following. Do you realize the father figure that has been on television the longest as of

2018 is Homer Simpson? He has been Hollywood's version of a "man" since December 17, 1989. Now, do you aspire to be Homer Simpson? Do you hope your son grows up to be Homer Simpson? I thought not.

We can look at our own fathers. By default, this is the first place a boy will look to see if he is, or can be, a man. Most research shows nearly 40 percent of babies born today are going to a home where there is no resident father. The question "Do I have what it takes to be a man?" is greeted by a deafening silence. Author John Eldridge ruminates a great deal about this question and why it goes unanswered for so many men and sons in his book, *Wild at Heart*. I encourage you to read it.

When we look at our own fathers, the problem is we are looking at an imperfect model. No matter how great your dad was, there were times he may have fallen short or missed the mark in leading you. As you grow and mature, you need to recognize his faults, but not use them as an excuse for your own poor behavior. You need to recognize them and forgive your dad. No matter the hurt. No matter the pain. You need to forgive him. Even if your dad has passed away, write him a letter and let him know you forgive him, a cathartic and liberating exercise.

Hebrews 12:10 says, *"They disciplined us for a short while as it seemed best to them ..."* As I grow and raise my own boys, I look back and can appreciate how difficult it must have been for my dad. I need to offer the same forgiveness to him I hope my boys will extend to me for the times when I fall short raising them. My dad died in 2009. Three weeks before he passed, I expressed that sentiment in a letter to him. While we were never able to talk about the letter, I am so thankful I did the hard work of writing it and overcame the fear of giving it to him.

However, there is one man we should absolutely be looking to as we work through what it means to lead courageously. His name is Jesus.

He is the model for our Manhood. He is the Guide we follow as we lead others. He is who we look to for behaviors, attitudes, and actions worth emulating. Jesus Christ was the greatest leader of all time. He had a ministry that lasted only three years yet, thousands of years later, he is the pivot point for our entire world.

We see Jesus and His model of leadership reported in Luke 22:24-27:

> *And He said to them, "The kings of the Gentiles exercise lordship over them, and those in authority over them are called benefactors. But not so with you. Rather, let the greatest among you become as the youngest, and the leader as the one who serves. For who is greater, one who reclines at the table, or one who serves? Is it not the one who reclines at the table? But I am among you as the one who serves."*

Jesus' model of leadership was a simple one. A courageous leader is one who serves.

Servant Leadership

We must fully embrace this idea of servant leadership. We have to understand it and strive to live it out every waking moment. We need to model it for our boys. We need to teach it to them constantly. We have to be a servant leader!

At its core, servant leadership means that I will leverage all I am and all I have for *you*. I will use my title, position, and authority to build you up and make you all God wants you to be. If I simply am out to gain more for myself, I may be leading, but doing it in such a way that *I* am the one to gain.

True servant leaders build up the people around them. They look for opportunities to elevate those around them. A servant leader will do his utmost to make those around him comfortable. Again, look at Jesus.

He spoke absolute truth. He was not afraid to tell people they were sinners. Nevertheless, sinners flocked to be near Him. Why? Because even though His message was unwavering, and He was not afraid to tell people they were wrong, He always did it out of love and He made them feel welcomed. We need to lead our family with that same heart. We need to lead them by serving and helping them as they go, not just pulling them along.

We need to be tough for our families, not tough on them.

We need to remember Ephesians 5:21 as we strive to be courageous leaders in the home. Paul calls for us to be *"submitting to one another out of reverence for Christ."*

We need to *lean in* to our family. We need to submit to them and serve them—not because they deserve it 100 percent of the time, but because we are **doing it for Christ!** His love for us should compel us to love our family so much we want to leverage all we have for all of them.

That is servant leadership. That is leading courageously. That is what our boys and our families need from us every single day.

Live Passionately

Life is far too short not to be passionate. In all that my boys do, I want them to be passionate. If there is passion for what we do, we are sure to think differently and lead courageously.

Without passion, work becomes a job. Without passion, marriage becomes a convenient living arrangement. Without passion, raising boys becomes exhausting.

The biggest key to living passionately is to know what you are living for. What is your purpose? What are you striving for? What do success and happiness look like to you?

What is your ending?

A Different Ending

I have fought the good fight, I have finished the race, I have kept the faith. Henceforth there is laid up for me the crown of righteousness, which the Lord, the righteous judge will award to me on that Day. (Timothy 4:7-8)

The Apostle Paul knew what was coming. He knew that soon the Romans would cut off his head for proclaiming the Good News of Jesus. Nevertheless, he also knew there was a reward waiting for him that was far greater than any this earth can offer.

That reward is important for us to remember as dads. We need to keep our eyes on the Eternal prize. Matthew Chapter 6 reminds us to *"lay up for yourselves treasures in heaven,"* not here on earth. We need to take that perspective with our kids.

We need to remember that things we do or do not do, say or

do not say, allow or do not allow will have long-lasting impacts. I want to have my grandchildren's children in mind as I raise my boys. I want to know the things I do now will have an impact long after I am gone. I want my life and my decisions to leave a legacy for generations to come.

I have had the honor of baptizing three of my sons (one to go). I may never have a daughter to walk down the aisle, but I have to believe the feeling of baptizing is very similar. I cannot express my joy in not only knowing they have placed their Eternal salvation in Jesus, but in the precious acts of standing next to them, telling them I love them, urging them to never forget this day, then lowering them into the water.

For me as a dad, this ceremony has been the pinnacle of my parenting. Having all my boys come to that saving knowledge of Christ is my ultimate goal. It is why God blesses us with children (Malachi 2:15).

However, it is so, so easy to take our eyes off our ultimate goal. We can so easily sacrifice divine purpose for what the rest of world tells us we should want for our children.

Comparison Trap

One of the biggest distractions from a dad's greater purpose is the comparison trap. We can be suckered into thinking that what other kids are doing matters. What other kids are involved in. What other kids get. This compulsion to compare shifts our focus away from what is most important—and, ultimately, it robs us of our passion. We can waste so much energy chasing things that do not matter that we have no energy to chase our heart's true passion.

When we compare our kids to other kids, we are not really comparing the kids; we are comparing ourselves to other dads. We cannot be outdone. We cannot let our kids miss out because that would be a poor reflection on us. In reality, we are still acting like we are in middle school and care more about what others think of us than making the best decision for our own kids.

We need to relinquish whatever people may think of us and make decisions that are best for our boys, our families, and ourselves! I have to be willing to let people think what they will of me. I have to be willing to lose friends. I have to be willing for my boys to lose friends. I have to be willing to defend my position.

If we buckle to peer pressure, to the fear of comparison, we will never be in a position where we can live with true passion toward the greater ending.

If I always choose the immediate reward, I miss out on the opportunity of legacy with my boys. I miss out on the opportunity to point them to Jesus and remind them that our home is not here (John 17:15-18). I miss the teaching moments to impress on them that we are not to just blithely go along with friends or culture. Jesus has so much more for us as His followers. If we think and act a little differently, we can know with certainty we are following where He wants to lead us (Romans 12:2). If I always choose the immediate reward, I will miss showing my boys how to live with true passion.

God has a great reward for me as a husband and father. Anything I can gain on this earth will pale in comparison to what is waiting for me on the other side of Eternity. I need to keep an Eternal perspective in all that I do; that is the ending I need to live toward with passion.

That Eternal perspective needs to be the filter through which I view my marriage, my kids, my job, my hobbies, how I spend my time, who my friends are, and every other facet of my life on this earthly plane. With that filter, the passion will flow.

I need to strive early and often to help my sons understand the ubiquitous comparison trap. It is hard to explain this idea to a 15-year-old, because he simply wants to fit in. I wish it were as easy as picking his friends. I cannot do that. However, I can help him understand that his choices in friends and in comparing himself to others can have permanent positive or negative impacts.

It's All Related

As you look back at my definition of Manhood, it is easy to see how these three pillars lean on each other. Without one, none are possible. If I am failing in one area, I will fail in all areas.

> *I have to **think differently** if I want to lead courageously and live passionately.*
>
> *I have to **lead courageously** if I want to think differently and live passionately.*
>
> *I have to **live passionately** if I want to think differently and lead courageously.*

With Kingdom impact as my ultimate goal and focus, these are pillars that I must consider and pursue every day. This is what I will call my boys toward. These are my foundation. As I walk, I will call my boys to follow me. I will not only teach them, but I will model for them what it means to be a man who has Kingdom impact on his friends, family, and community by thinking differently, leading courageously, and living passionately!

Breakfast Discussion

QUESTIONS FOR DADS:

1. What does it mean to you to think differently?

2. What does it mean to you to lead courageously?

3. What does it mean to you to live passionately?

4. If you were to write a definition of Manhood, what would it be?

QUESTIONS FOR SONS:

1. What do you think it means to be a man?

2. Based on what you know Manhood is, think about your friends. Which friends are helping you get closer to Manhood? Which are keeping you from it?

QUESTION FOR BOTH:

What is the one thing from this chapter that stands out to you and what will you do differently in the future?

Sentence 4

YOUR GUIDES

In case I did not have the chance to show you how to live like that, I have a group of men that will show you and they are men you can look to as Guides to follow.

Hit by a Bus

In today's world, there is almost no excuse not to be prepared for the worst. We should all have life insurance and other end-of-life policies set up. You can create your own Living Will or Last Will and Testament. You can pre-pay for and pre-plan your funeral. You can buy car insurance with little effort online. You can build a bomb shelter and stock it with food and supplies for the nuclear fallout of the last Great War.

It is a good thing to be prepared.[1]

When I began to think about my boys and the letter I wanted to write them, I realized that I had no plan in place to actually *show* them how to be man if, for whatever reason, I was not around to do it. I needed to create a plan so if the proverbial bus hit me, my boys would still know what it means to be a man, and know when they are men. I plan to be the one to show them, but I prepare in case I cannot be.

Certainly my call to Manhood will include them helping their brothers get there (that is the next sentence in my letter), but I need other men to help my boys too in case I am no longer around.

They will need some additional Guides.

If you don't have them

Earlier, I talked about the importance of having a mentor and accountability partners. Other men to lean on, share with, listen

---

[1] A bomb shelter for the zombie apocalypse might make you appear crazy. Just don't open the hatch when those neighbors come knocking. (Who's crazy now?)

to, challenge, and be challenged by. Men to walk this path with. Some of mine are friends from long ago and others I have connected with more recently. Regardless, they are men to whom I relate. I understand them and they understand me. They would be the four men I would tap to be Guides for my boys and they have accepted that responsibility. They are my accountability partners.

If I had not done the work required to build those relationships, having open conversations about my own struggles, beliefs, desires, and comfort levels, my boys would be in trouble.

Think about it. If you knew that tomorrow your life would end, to whom would you reach out *today* to stand in the gap for you with your family? Do you have someone, or a couple of men, who could do that? Do you know them well enough? What they believe? How they are raising their kids? How they love their wife? What their personal spiritual walk is?

If you know the answers to all of those questions, do you agree with them and would you be okay if they brought those values to your family?

If you do not have men like that in your life, you have no one to ask to serve as a Guide. Here is the good news: Getting men like that into your life as accountability partners is just as easy as getting a mentor. All you have to do is ask!

Men in general are terrible at opening up with other men, but our need for meaningful relationships is no less important than women's. We have just suppressed it and labeled it as "unnecessary" for "real men." That is a tragedy. We were created to interact in deep, meaningful, and emotional (yes, emotional) ways with other men.

Proverbs 27:17 tells us, *"Iron sharpens iron, and one man sharpens another."*

We need other men in our life. We need them for our sake. We need them for the sake of our boys.

Let's do breakfast

In reality, unless you have completely isolated yourself, you have already done the foundational work needed to have this kind of meaningful relationship. You already have this type of man around you.

You watch ball games with them. You coach Little League teams with them. You work with them. You have superficial conversations with them all the time. All it takes to make those relationships more meaningful is the guts to ask.

"Accountability groups" or "discipleship groups" do not need to be complicated or highly structured. You simply need to ask a couple of those men to meet for breakfast just to have a conversation about work, life, or whatever. As I said in an earlier chapter, you can decide to read a book in which you have a common interest. You could decide to read a chapter of the Bible and talk about it every week. It does not need to be onerous. It only needs to be approached with a genuine desire to make friends. Time will grow those friends into the kind of men you can someday call Guides.

Guiding Your Guides

As I said, I have called on four men to be Guides.

They are my friends. I have traveled a long road with them. They know how I define Manhood. They know what I am calling my boys towards. They know how I plan to do that, and I keep them in the loop as I plan. They will be involved in the ceremonies I will have for my boys. My boys will know them as more than just "some of Dad's buddies." It will be clear to my boys that these men are playing a special role in their lives.

I was intentional about reaching out to these four men when I realized that I, like you, like anyone, might need some Guides to stand in the gap for me.

It was a face-to-face conversation. I was clear in what I was asking of them. I was clear with my expectations of them.

Think of how serious the conversation was when you asked someone to be a Godparent or raise your kids if you and your wife were killed, or if someone asked you to fill that role for them.[2] My conversation with my four male friends was just as serious. It included everything I am writing about in this book.

They know the areas of life that I want my boys to see modeled, understood, and have a passion for. How the Guides do that will vary by Guide, vary by son, and a dozen other factors. But I know that, as Guides, there will be consensus on exactly how they want to work together to implement their roles and responsibilities.

While I do not necessarily expect the Guides to adopt my sons into every aspect of life, there is a clearly communicated expectation they will stand in the gap of my absence for my boys in a few key areas, even if (or when!) my wife remarries.

---

[2] You do have someone listed in your will to raise your kids if you and your wife die, right? If not, put down this book and go do it. Seriously. Stop reading. Go. Now.

Manhood

I want my Guides to explain my definition of and call my boys to Manhood. They know how I define it. They will teach it to my boys. They will guide them through the ceremonies in my place. It will be a collective effort with all four men playing that role.

As I continue to develop my plan in calling my sons, I will keep my Guides updated. They will know my heart's desire for my boys. As Guide, it will be their responsibility to impress all those things onto my children.

I want my boys to look to them to see what it looks like to strive after Kingdom impact by thinking differently, leading courageously, and living passionately. I want them to see men who are fighting for all the right things. Everything I would model for them, I want them to see in the Guides. I want them to have Guides they can go to with questions about how a man should handle a situation at home, school, or work.

Mom

These men will not only stand in the gap with my boys, but also with my wife. They will interject themselves into her life. They will help make sure she is cared for and protected, just as if I were here. They will be men she can call on when something at the house breaks. They will be men she will call when she needs help with a son who just won't listen.

This does not mean my wife cannot care for herself. Hardly! She is one of the most self-sufficient women I know.[3] She is strong.

---

[3] If you thought I was going to use any other description than "self-sufficient," you're a person who plays with fire.

She is powerful. She is everything a mom of four boys needs to be! However, if I am not here, there is no doubt a gap in her life. While these Guides will not be able to fill every void, I want them to step in where they can and wherever she needs them to.

Even as they fill voids for my wife, they are modeling for my boys. If I want my boys to honor, respect, and love their mom, if I am gone, they will need to see other men honor, respect, and love their mom.

Love and Marriage

If something were to happen to me, whether unexpected or through genetics, I am convinced my wife would someday remarry. She is too beautiful, smart, and sexy not to remarry![4] My boys will not be able to fend off all the men at her door—although I expect them to keep questionable suitors away.

Whether she remarries or not, the Guides have a role to play in modeling what love looks like. They are all married. I want my boys to see them within their marriages. I want my boys to see what loving and leading looks like in their homes.

I want them to see the husband "dying to self" and loving his wife. I want them to see a man who leads like Jesus, by being a servant. I want them to see the expectations I talk about in sentences six and seven in my letter, lived out in the flesh.

Plus, until my wife does remarry, I want them to see a God-honoring marriage in action. That involves not only how the Guide acts, but how his wife responds. I want them to see what to look for in a Godly woman. Yes, they have their mother as a

---

[4] Shameless attempt at bonus points. Don't judge.

shining example but, without me there, there may be marriage interactions they will only be able to witness while sitting at the kitchen table of one of their Guides.

Maintaining Guide Status

Raising boys up is a long process. As long as I am here, it will be my job. I will not carry it alone. I have my wife and my Guides to lean on and assist me. However, just because I have called on these four men now does not mean I will always call on them.

As the leader of the group that will lead my boys to Manhood, I have a responsibility to make sure I leave them in safe hands. This means I cannot ask a man to guide and then not maintain a relationship with him. I have to stay engaged in his life. I need him to stay engaged in mine. But friendships can drift, in one season, out another. That is fine for friends. It is not fine for Guides.

At any moment, a Guide may be needed. It is my job to make sure the Guides I have called on are always ready to be Guides. It is my job to make sure they are still up to the task. If they are not, that is fine. If I have other men who are more qualified, or become closer friends, that is fine. But I am the one who carries the responsibility to make sure my Guides know they are Guides and are ready when called upon.

Think of it as being like the flight attendant who comes up to you when you are seated in the emergency row and asks, "In case of an emergency, are you willing and prepared to assist me?" I need to do that with my Guides. They also need to understand and embrace the responsibility and accountability that comes with being a Guide. If, at any time, one begins to live a life that is counter to how I want my boys raised, his status as Guide can be modified or revoked.

As I sit here writing, I realize it has been over a year since I have had that conversation with my Guides. Would you like to guess what I am going to do within the next week?

The only people more important than you and your wife in raising your boys are the men you ask to raise them in your place. The Guides whose shoulders you tap will play a crucial role in the lives of your sons. They will be a part of the foundation you build on as you call your boys to Manhood. Should they need to fill your gap, they will use *your* life as the foundation they build on as they call your boys to Manhood.

Either way, the role they play in your life, the life of your wife, and the lives of your boys is critical.

Choose wisely. Choose carefully.

But please, choose.

And if you're not sure where to start, check out the Dear Boys Extra, *Five Rules for Choosing Guides*, at the end of the chapter.

DEAR BOYS EXTRA
Five Rules for Choosing Guides

I know that having the right Guides is critical. I also know that many men have no idea where to start when it comes to identifying and asking other men to play such a pivotal role. Let me share my five rules for choosing wisely.

1. Guides should be in various stages of life – If you are 42 years old with kids in middle school, all your Guides should not be men in their early forties with middle-school-age kids. The men should be in, and represent, different life stages. That will allow diverse perspectives to be shared with your boys.

2. They do not have to be family – If something happens to you and you have men in your family (brothers, grandparents, and the like), they may want to and should be able to influence your boys. Nevertheless, do not feel compelled to make them a Guide. When you have a clear direction you are calling your boys, any man who is not invested in that calling and living it out should never be a Guide, even if you are related.

3. Look for courage – If Guides are needed because of my death, I need men of great courage. It will require them stepping into delicate and tense situations with my wife and my boys. It is not for the faint of heart. Find men who are fearless, firm, and show fortitude.

4. Ask your wife – Your wife should have input as to who the Guides will be. She will be the one working with and calling

on them. She has to trust them. She has to find them relatable and dependable. She should have a say in the men you are proposing.

5. Simply ask – The scariest part about this whole process is the notion of sitting down with potential Guides and asking them. I would get all of them together at once and have the conversation. A group will be easier than one-on-one, and facilitate the Guides getting to know each other. Sit them down and share your vision for Manhood for your sons. Ask directly whether they will be willing to stand in the gap if something were to happen to you. You can have more conversations later. All you are looking for initially is a "yes."

I know the idea of Guides may be foreign to you and probably daunting, but I promise you that on this journey to Manhood for your sons, having men committed to stepping in on your behalf is critical and highly comforting.

Breakfast Discussion

QUESTIONS FOR DADS:

1. What do you have in the way of a living will, life insurance, and other plans in case something happens to you?

2. Who are the men you meet with regularly to hold you accountable?

3. If you were to pick four Guides today, who would they be? Why? When are you going to officially ask them to be a Guide?

QUESTIONS FOR SONS:

1. Do you think it's important for men to have other men in their lives? Why?

2. If you were to pick three friends to meet with regularly, who would they be? Why? It would be a great idea for you to start now!

QUESTION FOR BOTH:

What is the one thing from this chapter that stands out to you and what will you do differently in the future?

Sentence Five

YOUR JOB

As you learn what it means to be a Godly man, I expect you to lead your brothers on this journey, as well as your sons, and grandsons.

Fight

Our house is never quiet. Never. With four boys, there are times when it feels more like the British House of Commons with all the yelling or even the Coliseum with gladiators fighting for honor and life. Our drywall has more than its fair share of dents, scratches, and holes and we have furniture I refuse to replace until I am sure my boys will not break or set fire to it!

Homes with boys are accustomed to "loud." Homes with boys are accustomed to wrestling, tests of strength, and horseplay in general. At times with brothers, it escalates beyond any of that and it becomes an all-out fight. Punches thrown. Pushes and shoves. Wrestling morphs into ultimate fighting that doesn't usually end until someone taps out or is satisfied he has made his point. Memorably.

I am not naive enough to think my boys will not have these kinds of skirmishes. In fact, even with only two teenagers as of now (so testosterone flow is still at a minimum), we occasionally encounter this. They do scuffle. They do get on each other's nerves.

Nevertheless, as time goes on and I guide them through this journey towards Manhood, I have an expectation of them: They will play an integral role in modeling what I am teaching. They will model that for their younger brothers and they will all hold each other accountable.

As they grow, I expect them to stop fighting with each other and start fighting *for* each other. I expect them to teach what they have been taught. I expect them to model what has been modeled. I do not want them to just rely on their authority as "older brother." I want them to influence the others as "older man." I want them to be actively involved in their younger siblings' journeys to Manhood.[1]

The older boys will be actively involved in the ceremonies of the younger. I want them to be able to share, in their own words, what they have heard me teach. I want them to use their wisdom, their experiences, and their insights to mold, shape, and encourage their younger brothers and each other. I want to create an environment for them as brothers to look to and lean on each other. My future grandsons will look to their dad and their uncles. My future granddaughters will look at Manhood played out not just by their dad, but by their uncles.

When done right, the family will become all that a family is supposed to be.

In fact, as I guide them along the journey, if they do not sincerely *want* to be involved as I guide their younger brothers, I will feel that I have done something wrong. My teaching and guiding should make it clear to them that they have a role to play in the Manhood journey of every other male within their family.

Legacy

The idea of brothers guiding brothers hints at and leans toward something beyond myself. I see it as an integral role for what I am called to with my sons. This call to have brothers guide brothers is my true legacy. My words and actions will live in my sons, in my grandsons, and beyond, long after I am gone.

---

[1] Yes, I know this means the youngest one gets a pass. But if you're the oldest child, like me, you know the youngest ones always do, right?

One day, my oldest will look at my youngest and say, "Like dad taught me ..." Or perhaps my youngest will look at his nephew and say, "Your grandpa would want you to know ..."[2] It is in those moments that my life continues. All I stood for, all I fought for, and all I prayed for will be imprinted on those who come after me.

Those future exchanges will be my true and lasting legacy.

When I am gone, I do not believe that people in general will still talk about me. However, I do hope that my family will. I hope they will take the things I shared and taught and pass them down. I really have only one chance to be remembered 100 years after I am gone, and it lies in how I raise my boys, how they will raise my grandsons, and how my great-grandsons will be raised. Pastor Andy Stanley has famously said, "The most important thing you do in this life may not be a 'what' but a 'who.'"

Exactly.

My boys are my legacy. My passion can live on in them. All I have learned from successes and failures dies with me, unless I am intentional about passing on those lessons.

Engaged vs. Intentional

I suppose now is a good time to talk about being intentional. It is an idea that is fundamental to everything we are discussing, but it becomes particularly important when we explore our legacy.

Let me ask you a question: Are you engaged or are you intentional with your boys?

---

[2] You really didn't think he would get a pass, did you?

How you answer that question makes a huge difference. Being intentional is nothing like being engaged. The difference between the two can sometimes be hard to distinguish. It can be easy to think you are being intentional, when you are really only being engaged.

This distinction, though, is one that can and should permeate all areas of your life, including not only raising your boys, but your friendships, marriage, and faith.

Let me illustrate the difference:

> *You are sitting on a plane ready to take a vacation on an island in the Caribbean. The flight attendant tells you the captain is the most experienced pilot in the entire company. He has logged more hours flying than any other. The captain comes over the speakers and says:*
>
> *"Good morning, folks. This is a great day to be flying. The sun is shining, visibility is perfect. Sit back, relax, and enjoy the flight."*
>
> *You settle into your seat, fully confident in his ability. After two hours in the air, he comes back on the intercom:*
>
> *"Folks, this is your captain again. We have been in the air for just over two hours. The weather conditions were perfect and all has gone well. Please prepare for landing."*
>
> *As the plane descends, you look out the window and become confused. The sights are very similar to what you saw when you took off. In fact, when the plane lands, you realize you are right back where you started.*

> *"Welcome back," the captain says cheerily over the intercom, "and thanks for flying with us today. We trust you've enjoyed it."*

Question: Was the captain engaged in the flight?

Of course he was. He handled the plane beautifully. He did all the things he needed to, to fly the plane safely. He was completely engaged.

Another question: Was the captain intentional in the flight?

No way! Had he been intentional, he would not only have done all the things he did when he was engaged, but he would have known where he was going and done the things necessary to get there.

Are you simply flying your life splendidly or do you have a destination in mind, making decisions and taking actions to ensure you arrive there?

Let me give you one sure-fire way to recognize you are simply engaged, but not intentional.

Look at your daily and weekly to-do list. Is there anything on it focusing on six, 12 or 24 months from now? If not, you may be engaged, but I'll bet you aren't being intentional. You need to do some long-term planning for your life, your legacy, and your boys. What do you want your boys to know a year from now? What is the date of their next ceremony? If you truly believe, as I do, that our boys are our legacy, you will work to guide them with a future mindset.

Being intentional takes far more effort than simply being engaged; there is no doubt about that. However, the results are more than worth the effort. Remember: Your legacy is your plane. Don't just fly it. Make sure it lands where you want it to.

Students become Teachers

If I am to achieve my goal of a long-lasting legacy, I have to teach my boys. I have to teach them not only my definition of Manhood, or how to be a Man, but how they need to teach Manhood. They need to know how to lead others along the same journey I am leading them on. I need to instill the desire and know-how for them to share all I teach them with their brothers and, later, their sons.

There are three ways I think about doing this as they grow.

Define, Then Embrace It

I have already talked at length about the definition of Manhood I plan to teach my sons. This idea of their job to be a Guide for their brothers falls under "lead courageously." If they are going to fully embrace Manhood, they need to lead others. There is no doubt that stepping into the life of their brothers, friends, or their own kids will require large doses of courage.

If they truly embrace my definition, or maybe even create one of their own someday, the proof will be in how well they can explain it to others. They have to be able to expound upon it with clarity and conviction. They have to be able to defend it to questions and scrutiny.

Have you ever asked someone why they believe something and it became very evident their belief was rooted not in their own personal sentiments but in someone else's thoughts? It is obvious someone taught them. They may even have it memorized. They may deliver the message with confidence. But when it comes to being able to explain and defend it, they come up short.

Giving my boys a definition of Manhood is a great place to start. A place from which to build. It is not the pinnacle of their journey; it is the base camp. It is the seed from which everything grows.

They have to embrace the intent and foundation of my definition. They need to live with it. They need to make it theirs. I am perfectly happy if they decide to change it. They can change it to their own words or even change it to what they want it to be. Each boy is uniquely created and designed. The greatest sign they are embracing the call to Manhood will be when they take what I am calling them to, understand it, embrace it, and maybe even adapt it.

Defining Manhood is the easy part.

Embracing it is a bit harder.

Live It

Living what they define and embrace is harder yet. As we've established, they will model what they see so I have to live it out in front of them.

Not only do I have to live it, but I also have to expect them to live it. There will be times I need to step back and let them take the lead in living it out. Let me share a favorite memory to drive this point home.

When I was 14, my family was returning from a Spring Break trip to Florida. It was early in the morning on an Easter Sunday. We had left Naples the day before and driven all night. It was early (like 4 a.m. early) and we were in Kentucky. We had just stopped outside Elizabethtown for gas. My mom and little brother were asleep in the back seat and I was riding shotgun.

My dad, who drove a truck as his career and was accustomed to life on the road, had been behind the wheel all night.

There is a 250-mile stretch of Interstate 65 between Elizabethtown and Louisville that, at the time, was three lanes. I mentioned that it was early Easter Sunday, right? The highway was empty. See where this is going?

My dad pulled over as we entered the interstate and said, "You're up." I looked at him, shocked and excited. I glanced back at my mom, sound asleep. I knew what I had to do. I had to get into the driver's seat. Quietly. Very quietly.

The next couple of hours were gold. I was BMOC[3], screaming north in our Mercury Sable. I was having so much fun. It was sheer, unadulterated bliss. Until mom woke up. We were all perfectly safe, so Dad had no idea why she was screaming.

I was young, yes, but I had understood driving. I had fully embraced the idea of driving, and what it meant to drive. It was time for me to live it and that is exactly what my dad had allowed me to do.

There will come times in the journey to Manhood when I will need to step back and let each of my boys live it. They will need to live it while I am watching. Then, I can coach, direct, support, and encourage.

Here are some practical ways that plays out in our family.

I ask them to pray before meals. I have them lead a devotional. The older ones will be involved when the younger ones are baptized. When we have ceremonies, the older ones will have a part to play.

---

[3] Big Man On Campus, Hot Stuff, Big Time, King of the World

I have to let them live out Manhood, even before they are men. They need to experience it.

After they define it, embrace it, and live it, there is one final key.

Expect It

My sons need to expect Manhood from each other. Expecting it from their brothers, sons, nephews, and others is the final action that shows their commitment. Only when they expect it from each other will they truly become teachers.

Notice how these four stages of going from student to teacher build on each other. You do not get to skip a step. Boys cannot embrace Manhood until they define it. Only when it is defined and embraced can they can live it out. They cannot expect it from others until they are living it out themselves. Expecting Manhood from each other demands a couple of things.

First, they must have the courage to speak that kind of truth to each other.[4] As brothers, they may not always want to listen to one another. They certainly won't always want to hear what another brother has to say about behavior, language, or decisions. They barely can stand that now! But if they are truly going to call others to Manhood, expecting others' actions to align with the calling is critical. If they see inconsistency, they cannot simply shrug it off, "Oh, I'm just going to let that go." They have to speak up.

They also need to have the courage to listen when they are called out. Being vulnerable enough to have someone challenge them is critical. If they are not willing to listen and take correction,

---

[4] Remember "Lead Courageously"? This is one place courage is needed!

they will have no credibility when it is time for them to challenge someone else. No one will ever get it right all day, every day. Sure, I expect them to strive for it every day, as I do, but we all will fall short. It is in those moments when they will need to listen to others point out shortcomings.

The ultimate proof that my boys fully embrace all I have called them and guided them to will be when they call and guide others.

I can't wait!

Breakfast Discussion

QUESTIONS FOR DADS:

1. Talk about a time when you fought for something.

---

2. What do you want your legacy to be? What do you want to be remembered for?

---

3. Think back to a time in your life as Dad when you were engaged, but not as intentional as you could have been. What was it and how would you change it if you could?

QUESTIONS FOR SONS:

1. What do you want your legacy to be? What do you want to be remembered for?

2. What is the scariest part to you about teaching someone else what it means to be a man?

3. If you have younger brothers, what is one thing you know you would like to teach them and help them understand about growing up?

QUESTION FOR BOTH:

What is the one thing from this chapter that stands out to you and what will you do differently in the future?

_____

_____

_____

_____

_____

_____

Sentences Six and Seven

YOUR WIFE

Even when you don't feel like it, love your wife and put her above everyone and everything else by dying to self and leading as a servant, because she is a Daughter of Christ. Remember, you are called to honor and love her and will be held accountable to God for how well you do that.

First This

Have you ever had something you knew you needed to do but, because it was going to be hard, you kept finding other things to do instead?[1]

That is how I have felt about this chapter. Of all the sentences in the letter, these are the two about which I feel the most unqualified to talk. These are the two I struggle to live out with the unerring consistency I wish I could. I am writing this chapter as the ideal I strive for every day and who I hope to be on my best day. I am not penning it from a position of, "Oh, look at me. I am a perfect model of a husband."

If it has been a while since you read Sentence 2 (Your Mom), you may want to go back and skim through it or at least refresh yourself on your answers to the questions. The words to my sons about their mom and their future wives are so closely tied, it is important to have the filter of the former as we embark on this.

There are two areas I need to mention before we delve into the two sentences. These two areas set the context in which to talk about marriage. They are both things my boys will need to understand and embrace if they someday will love their wives well.

On Being Single

In Jesus' time, there was a stigma attached to those who were unmarried and those who didn't have kids. Young adults today are waiting longer to tie the knot and start a family. Inside the

---

[1] Procrastinators, unite! Tomorrow.

Western Christian faith, though, there still is somewhat of a stigma for someone in their late twenties or early thirties who isn't in a serious (soon-to-be-engaged) dating relationship. That stigma is usually placed on them by well-meaning adults over the age of 50 who can't imagine being 28, unmarried and childless. At 28, they were married and had two kids because that was the "way it was done." They graduated high school, maybe went to college, got married by 23, and began procreating. That path is a familiar one even for me.

However, I want my boys to know that my path does not have to be their path when it comes to marriage. Yes, I pray often for their spouses-to-be. I pray they fall deeply in love and take vows. So much of this life is made beautiful by having a Godly wife to share it with. (My wife is already excited about all the grandbabies four sons should produce. She envisions her late fifties and beyond being spent as a professional grandbaby watcher. Oh, and if some could be girls, that would be a bonus!)

I have to remind myself that Jesus was single. He never married. He lived life to its fullest and fulfilled every purpose His Father called Him to and that did not include a wife or kids. I want my boys to be secure and confident in the men God has created and called them to be. They need to know that if that calling does not include a wife, so be it.

I have to remind myself that there is nothing wrong if they aren't in serious relationships at 25, just because I was married at 23. In fact, if they are chasing after Christ, I don't ever want to them to stop that because it's "time to settle down." Their path to marriage won't be my path. (More on that in the next section.)

Having a spouse to go through life with is wonderful. Having a partner beside you as you strive for Kingdom impact is a true gift from God. Having children to raise is an awesome blessing—and an awesome challenge.

However, none of those things are necessary to live a full life. None of those things are prerequisites to living a life that honors God. If any of my boys do not have the desire to marry, or if marriage isn't something God has in mind for them, I need to be fine with that. My wife needs to be fine with that, too.

The Dating Game

I am so thankful that I do not have to date in today's society. Technology and social media make dating today almost unimaginably different than when I was young. I did not have a broad dating life. My wife, Amber, is the only woman I ever had a serious relationship with. We met in high school. She was a year older than I was and we went to her senior prom together. We dated through the rest of my time in high school and my four years of college. I graduated on a Saturday in May 1999. She graduated the next day. The following Saturday we were married. It was a busy week!

That path worked out tremendously for me. It could work out for my boys, too. But it is not the only path. In fact, I want them to make sure they are confident in who they are and were created to be before they fall in love and place some of their identity, hopes, and dreams in another person.

There are some great resources and books on dating. I do not need to re-create the wheel here and I plan to use some of those resources as my boys approach dating age.

That's 16, by the way. My boys need to be 16 before they can undertake any kind of serious dating relationship. I know, I know.

There is nothing stopping them from having a girlfriend at 14. Sure, they could hang out at lunch, ball games, and dances. But they will be 16 before I will allow them to go anywhere alone with a girl. They will be 16 before I will allow a girl to come over to the house or one of my boys to go over to a girl's house.[2]

Why 16? Simple. By then, they will have been through this book with me. We will have had countless conversations about Manhood, how to live, how to treat women, and what is important when thinking about dating or marriage. Oh, and don't worry. We have already had the "sex talk" and covered the importance of what God calls us to as it relates to our bodies. (See the Dear Boys Extra, *Four Rules for Boys and the "Talk"*, at the end of this chapter.)

A couple more quick thoughts on dating. It is really important that as my boys think about it, they think about it as preparation for marriage. This means they should really only consider being in any serious relationship with someone who shares the same profession of faith. Their faith should be foundational to everything they do in life, including dating.

I also want them to remember what they are chasing: Kingdom impact. I want them to chase after Christ, making impact for His Kingdom. When they find a woman who can keep up with that chase, they should treasure her and make it permanent.

How they treat their girlfriends will be an early indication of how they will treat their wives. I want each of my sons to date in a way that honors his commitment to Christ. Because of how

---

[2] As I think about my oldest doing those things within 15 months, I almost get sick to my stomach anticipating dealing with all that fun.

he treats her, she should be encouraged to grow in her personal faith, whether she marries him or not.

There is a lot in those last three paragraphs. There is a lot of conversation to be had about dating. That is exactly why I included them here. The stage is set for a conversation and I will get to have one over breakfast sometime soon!

The Hardest Thing

Being married is hard. It is fun. It is joyful. It is wonderful. But it is hard.

Beyond helping my boys define and be called to Manhood, I believe the best thing I can do for them is help them understand the mindset, attitude, and heart needed to enter marriage. I want to frame the marriage mindset by looking at the verse I view as the foundation for how I am to live as a husband. 1 Peter 3:7 says, "Likewise, husbands, live with your wife in an *understanding way*, *showing honor* to the woman as the weaker vessel, since *they are heirs* with you of the grace of life, so that your *prayers may not be hindered*."

Before I explain the four key ideas in that verse (italics mine), let me address the elephant in the room. It's the line that says woman is the "weaker vessel." The Apostle Peter is simply reminding us that, in most cases, the wife isn't going to win a boxing match against her husband. In a society where statistics show physical, sexual, verbal, and emotional abuse of women is rampant, Peter's words have never rung more true.[3] So let's

---

[3] If you don't believe me, check out ncadv.org (the National Coalition Against Domestic Violence). Men, we should be ashamed of ourselves.

not miss out on all this verse has to teach us and our sons about loving our wives because of that one phrase.

Love

At the heart of this verse, while not explicitly mentioned, is the idea that we are to love our wives. Love is the thread holds the whole verse together. In fact, Peter's good friend and fellow disciple, Paul, wrote a letter to the Church in Ephesians wherein he reminds us as husbands that we are to love our wives as Christ loved the Church. Spoiler alert: That means we must be willing to die for them (Ephesians 6).

I think back to when Amber and I were going through the airport on our way home from our honeymoon in St. Thomas. Remember, we had dated for over five years before we were married. We were chatting with a security guard and we mentioned we were newlyweds. "That's nice," he said. "I can see you have that newlywed glow." Without missing a beat, I looked at him and joked, "Nah. That's just sunburn."

Love is a funny thing. So many people think it's that warm, fuzzy, weak-kneed feeling you get when you are around someone. It is true that deep love can cause a physical response in your body. So can bad pizza. Love is so much more than a feeling. If you have been married for over a year, you know there are times you don't feel like loving your wife.

We have to remember that our commitment to love our wives is a mindset and choice we make daily, even when the feeling of love is absent. There are moments in the craziness of life when you wonder if you even *like* your wife, but you know you must always choose love. Let me give you two suggestions for when you've lost that loving feeling.

First, learn the mantra *"die to self."* One of the main reasons we stop showing love to someone else is because we begin to focus on ourselves. We begin to think about all the things *I want* or *I deserve*. In those instants, we lose sight of the person who should be the focus of our love, intentions, and actions: our wife. Anytime I feel *self* rising up within me, I say over and over, *"Die to self. Die to self. Die to self."* If I am going to love my wife well, if my boys are going to see me model what a husband looks like, I need to wrest the day away from *self*.

The second idea is born out of the first: the idea of being a servant leader. Yes, I need to lead my family. Yes, I need to lead in the marriage. However, I need to do that with the mindset of a servant leader. I need to be willing to leverage everything I have and everything I am for the good of my wife. I need to sacrifice so she succeeds. I need to defer so she can decide. I need to ensure she has everything she needs from me, so she can be all God has called her to be. I need to follow the model of Jesus and be the one to wash the feet. I need to serve.

Dying to self and thinking like a servant leader are mandatory if I am going to love my wife, especially on those days when I do not feel like loving her! Especially on those days when it would be easier to just worry about myself, my needs, and my wants. After all, taking care of self is always the easier (and sometimes more gratifying) thing to do.

Dying to self and having the mindset of a servant definitely make marriage healthier and more harmonious.

An Understanding Way

Any time I study Scripture, I like to look at various translations and even a concordance to see what the word(s) meant in the original language. For 1 Peter 3:7, the English Standard Version uses the phrase "understanding way." The New International Version says, "... be considerate as you live with your wives ..." The New Living Translation says, "...treat your wife with understanding as you live together." The King James tells us to "... dwell with them according to knowledge." All very similar wording.

When you look up the verse in Strong's Concordance, the Greek word used has the connotation that we should know our *wives (absolutely) in a great variety of applications and with many implications; be sure.*[4]

Whatever the translation, the idea is that we need to work at getting to know our wives. We need to know them deeply, who God has called them to be. We need to know what they like, what they don't like. We need to order their favorite drink at Starbucks without asking them to text it to us so we get it right.

A great way to better understand our wives is to talk with them. I know. What a shocking suggestion.

All joking aside, we must actively and intentionally engage them in conversation about what is going on in their world, in their minds. Do you know what your wife prays for at night? Asking her is a great way to get to know her better. When you go out to dinner, are you asking questions about her life, what's on

---

[4] Strong's Concordance offers a great app to study Greek words and meanings, especially if you know absolutely zero about biblical Greek language, like me.

her heart, what her hopes and dreams are? Or are you scrolling through social media on your phone and talking more to the waiter?

Our boys need to see us working to understand their mothers, because it is what they will need to do as they date and marry. I do not have to tell you that women do not act and think like men.[5] To live with our wives in understanding ways, we have to do more than just trust our (manly) instincts. If we are going to live with them in a way that allows us to do the other things 1 Peter 3:7 calls us to, we have to truly know them.

Honor

This is where the conversation about Sentence Two (*Your Mom*) and this section overlap. In that earlier chapter, I talked about what honor looks like. Take a couple of minutes and go back to reread the section *Honor Her* on page 64.

No, really. Go back and reread it.

Here is one sentence from that section: "Honor is looking at a person and thinking, 'Wow.' It is holding that person in such regard that when it comes to conflicting wants, you yield."

Funny how reading that sentence about honor ties so closely to the previous section about love, dying to self, and servant leadership. Do you see how if you aren't loving your wife, dying to your own wants, and serving her, it will be nearly impossible to honor her? Like so many other things with raising our boys, everything builds on everything else. It is all so intertwined and

---

[5] So many jokes here. However, my wife will read this book, so did you really think I was going to make one?

interdependent that you cannot get away with paying a lot of attention to the areas you like and little to the hard ones. You must make an effort at every area of this journey.

Heirs

This phrase, "since they *are heirs* with you of the grace of life" is a reminder of the seriousness of my role in loving my wife. Remember my earlier story about my son running down the hallway in the mornings yelling, "My princess," to wake up and kiss his mom?

Turns out, he was right. She really is a princess and the daughter of a King. As I think about loving, honoring, and living to better understand my wife, I need to remember she is an heir in the kingdom of heaven first.

I need to not only know *who* she, but *whose* she is.

She is a daughter of Christ. She has a relationship with her Savior and heavenly Father. In order of priority and importance in life, I am not the most important person and neither should the kids be. She should be chasing Christ, searching for the will of her Father in heaven. As she does that, I should be helping her be everything the King wants her to be.

Here is the question to ask: Is the relationship between my wife and Christ growing *because of* or *in spite of* how I am loving and leading her?

If it is not growing because of my actions, I am failing in my role as head of the family. I am certainly not loving her the way Christ loved the Church. I need to be creating a home where she wants to get closer to Christ. Here are some practical questions to see how we are doing:

- Am I leading spiritual conversations in the home?
- Do I initiate prayer with my wife and boys daily?
- Am I keeping the family engaged in a local church and Bible study?
- Does my wife ask me to pray for her?
- Am I creating time and space for my wife to have quiet time, read her Bible, and/or attend a Bible study?

That is far from an exhaustive list, but you get the idea. My wife is a *fellow heir* in Christ and I have married a princess. I need to make sure I am loving and leading her in a way that makes her Father, the King, proud.

A Final Warning

Peter ends this verse with a not-so-happy warning. He tells us if we fail to love, honor, and understand our wife, or treat her as a fellow heir, that our prayers will be *hindered*. Literally that our prayers will be *cut off* from God.

Picture God with His fingers in his ears, singing "Nah, nah, nah, nah," while you pray. He simply is not listening to you.

When I talk with men who tell me they feel frustrated with their spiritual life or direction, my first question is how their relationship with their wife is going. If it is not going well, I tell them to start there. Repair that. Ask her for forgiveness. Get right with her and, in the process, you'll get right with God.

I believe Peter's stern warning is a direct reflection of the idea that our wives truly are daughters of the King first. How many of you would expect your earthly father-in-law to support, listen to or help you if you were treating his daughter poorly? If you were being selfish and putting your needs over hers? If you showed no respect for the person she is? Why would he want to engage with you at all, when you treat his daughter that way?

How much more does our heavenly Father love our wives? Immeasurably. Failing to love our wives in the ways God calls us to has real consequences—and not just earthly ones.

A Final Encouragement

At the beginning of this chapter, I said I had been dreading writing it because of how hard it was going to be. Well, my dread was well founded. As my computer sat on my desk for the last three days, I would sit to write, begin, get lost in my thoughts, walk away, come back, peck away some more. Thankfully, I have an amazing editor, so you will never know how garbled and schizophrenic this chapter initially was.

I now know why this chapter was so hard and weighed so heavily on my heart. It's this: my boys' marriages will be the most impactful earthly relationships they will have. Marriage will stretch and change them in ways they can never imagine. It could literally be the greatest thing in their lives. It could inspire them to perform noble acts, small or large, and be one of their greatest legacies. It could also be the opposite of all that.

That is the importance of me modeling it and teaching it to my boys. That is why it takes up two of my 10 sentences.

That is the importance of me getting this right.

That is the importance of you getting this right.

DEAR BOYS EXTRA
Four Rules for Boys and the "Talk"

I am often asked about when I have the sex talk with my boys. I have broken it down into four basic rules. Once "the talk" is over, I use relevant moments to remind them about or reinforce the things we discussed.

1. I have the talk – The talk about sex is not one my wife has with the boys. I do. I initiate the conversation. I lead the conversation. Yes, she will engage in a conversation with them, but not until they are dating (she is their first date). "Go ask your mom," is not an appropriate answer to a question about sex, dads.

2. Start young – The conversation needs to begin sooner than you think. You don't need to have it in its entirety when they are nine years old, but it should start then. The summer my sons turn nine, I take them with me to Northwest Ontario on a fishing trip. One afternoon, while sitting in the boat, I have a simple conversation with them about pornography. Now, I don't even use that word. I simply talk about what should happen if someone were to show them pictures of people without clothes on. We handle it just as we do guns: Get away. Tell an adult. Tell me. That's it. It lasts less than five minutes. We haven't taken the plunge, but we have taken a dip.[6]

---

[6] The average age boys are exposed to porn: 11 (digitalkidsinitiative.com). I want my sons to hear it from me first. Like I said, "start young."

Sentences Six and Seven **YOUR WIFE**

3. Here's your cue – Watch your boys closely. You will know when they are ready for a deeper conversation based on what they do during movies. When you are coming to a kissing scene in *Star Wars,* do they start to talk nervously, cover their eyes, or lean in closer? That means they know exactly what is going on and it is time to talk more about sex. That moment will be different for each son, based on his maturity.

4. Tell them everything – Our boys are in public school so we use the videos they show in Grade 5 as a conversation starter. However, when the time comes for the full conversation, it is long and in depth. By the end, there is nothing relating to sex that my 12-year old could see or hear from a friend that he and I did not cover. We talk about our own bodies and changes coming. We talk about sex. We talk about porn. We talk about everything. Everything. Yes, even that.

Breakfast Discussion

QUESTIONS FOR DADS:

1. Talk about what made you fall in love with your wife. What made you want to date her and marry her?

2. Talk about a time when you showed your wife love, when you really didn't feel like it.

3. What words of wisdom do you have for your son about dating and marriage?

QUESTIONS FOR SONS:

1. What is the scariest thing about dating?

2. When have you seen your dad honoring and leading your mom well?

QUESTION FOR BOTH:

What is the one thing from this chapter that stands out to you and what will you do differently in the future?

Sentences Eight and Nine

YOUR SAVIOR

Most importantly, recognize your need for the Savior, Jesus Christ. Remember that His gift is about Grace (not about being perfect or trying to earn anything), about accepting the gift of Jesus, and then chasing Him your entire life—it is the most important thing you can do.

The Most Important Decision

What I know of ancient history, what I know of ancient literature, and what I have experienced in my own life tells me there is no question more important than this one:

Who was Jesus Christ?

No one argues He lived. No one argues He died. No one argues He was a great teacher and started a movement that is still thriving 2,000 years later. However, to me, He was more than that. He was God in flesh. He died on a cross and defeated death by being raised three days later. Because of that sacrifice, I have to make things right with a just and holy God who demands payment for sin.

I was raised in the Christian faith; I come from a long line of believers. For most of my childhood, I remember going to church regularly. I attended Sunday school, vacation Bible school, youth group, and church camp.

I asked Jesus to be my Savior in June of 1991, at a church camp in Grand Rapids, MI on the campus of Calvin College. I was 14 years old. I was baptized in 1993 at the First Missionary Church in Berne, IN.

Faith has always been a part of my life, but it has not always been the focus of my life. In fact, until I was 26 I would have described myself as a lukewarm, worldly Christian at best. Yes, I went to church. I prayed. I talked about God. I did it, though, in the way someone does because it is the cultural or "right" thing to do, not because he is truly living it. Then, when I was 26, something happened that shook me to my core and made me realize it was time to take my faith and my daily relationship with Christ seriously.

In May of 2003, my first son was born. That was the tipping point. I began to live with intention.

Needless to say, from 2003 on, I have not been perfect. Some of the worst decisions in my life were made after that moment. I have had to confess more than my share of sin, and ask forgiveness from my Savior, my wife, my kids, and my friends. I decide daily to lean into His Word and His will for my life. It is never easy and I do not always get it right, but I will always strive to live out my faith in a real way.

Being a child of God is where my identity lies. It is the foundation for everything I do and aspire to teach my boys. I want them to see me genuinely live out my faith, even when that means I struggle or sometimes fail. My identity in Christ sets direction for my actions. It sets filters for my decisions.

Recognizing my need for a Savior and professing Christ as my Lord was the most important decision I have ever made. It is also the most important decision my sons could ever make. As of today, I am beyond grateful that all four of my boys have trusted Jesus as their Savior. The three eldest have all been baptized and my youngest will be baptized in the coming months.

Grace, No Matter What

I want my boys to have a strong work ethic. I want them to know how to put in a hard day's work and feel good about that effort. I want them to realize that anything is possible with determination, hard work, and focus.

Well, almost anything.

Grace. The Google definition is, *"(in Christian belief) the free and unmerited favor of God, as manifested in the salvation of sinners and the bestowal of blessing."*

In a world where society ascribes value to what you do and how well you do it, Grace is counter-cultural. I desperately want my boys to understand the idea of *unmerited favor*, because it is such a freeing idea. It is also something I struggle with. I have always been driven and love to feel like I have achieved and accomplished. However, this drive has always created tension within me; I believe in Grace intellectually, but act like I have to work my way into heaven.

I should absolutely work hard and I should absolutely work hard for Kingdom impact. If I allow that work to become the focus and foundation of my faith, though, I begin a slippery slope to a faulty way of thinking and false doctrine. With a mindset of work, I never find peace. I never find rest. I never find Grace. Worse still, my boys see that mindset in my words and actions. If I want them to know they have a heavenly Father who loves them no matter what they do (or do not do), they need an earthly father to model it.

Candidly, this mindset has already caused me shame and my boys harm. When I am critical of every action because it was not "right," they see work-based love. When a chore they do is not good enough, I am saying to them, "If you want my full love, you need to do better." I want to challenge them to do their best. I want them to be accountable for their work and their effort. I have a leadership philosophy that speaks to this idea: hard on results, soft on people.

The same idea applies to my boys: hard on the results, soft on the boys. When I am hard on the results and the boys, they begin to equate the good work with love.

> *"For by grace you have been saved through faith.
> And this is not your own doing; it is the gift of God,
> not a result of works, so that no one may boast."*
> (Ephesians 2:8-9)

It could not be clearer than that. I need to show my boys daily that I love them, no matter what, no matter their works. I do not want them to feel like they need to *boast about working hard so I love them.* I need to offer them Grace when they fail. I need to offer Grace and forgiveness, just like my heavenly Father has offered Grace to me (over and over and over again).

If I truly want to be in a position to talk to my boys about their faith, I need to show them the love of the Father. If I want them to grow up with a deep faith and love for Christ, I need to show them I love them simply because they are mine, and not because of what they do or do not do.

I need to show them Grace, no matter what.

A Faith Worth Having

Their decision to accept Jesus Christ is the most important and first step. But I am not naïve enough to think the work is done. In fact, the real work for them (and me as their dad) is just beginning, as I now want to make their profession of faith as real to them as possible. I want it to be something they will not only carry with them, but grow deeply into in the years ahead. There are two main ideas I want to share with them as they learn what it means to be a follower of Christ: 1) I want them to take my faith and make it their own; 2) I want them to profess their faith and fully possess it.

Here is what you need to know. These ideas are not new. In fact, I bet many of you have used these ideas with your kids, to love other things in life. At the end this chapter, I will give you an example that you should be able to relate to and you will see exactly what I am talking about played out.[1]

Taking and Making

When my boys were younger, if you were to ask me why I went to church, one of the top reasons would have been because I wanted my sons to get into the habit of going.

Yes, I love corporate worship. I enjoy hearing a challenging message. I revel in connecting with other believers in conversation. But, as importantly, I wanted my boys to know that getting up on a Sunday morning and going to church was just something we did. I wanted them to *take* my faith.

Before they would ever be able to understand the Christian faith, they would be able to see me live it out. Before they could ever claim that faith as their own, I had to put them in a position to do so. We got to that position by repetition. We would go. Every week. They to their worship experience, we to ours. Sometimes they sat with us. They would tag along when we worshipped, when we served, when we went to small group.

Young kids might not understand all that is going on but they quickly learn, because of the importance you place on it, that church is part of who they are. I truly want my kids to be

---

[1] Fair warning—It will be a sports analogy and if you are a Cleveland Browns fan, you may be offended. You will definitely get the point, but you may not like it.

able to say, "I grew up a Christian in a Christian home."

If I truly give them a faith to *take*, from there I need to help them *make* it their own. What I cannot do is try to have the way I live out my faith be the way they live out their faith.

Why not? Simple. We are not the same person. God has different plans for our lives and He has given different gifts to accomplish those plans. If my boys take my faith and then try to fit the way I live it out into their lives, I foresee that by the time they are 20, they will drop it and walk away. No, they need to grow into their faith. They need to read the Bible and see what Truth God has for them. I need to help, guide, counsel, and challenge. Simply "doing it like I do" is not the best plan.

I want them to make the Christian faith theirs. Fully. There is a great line from the Apostle Peter's letter where he is talking about suffering for the faith: *"but in your hearts honor Christ the Lord as holy, always being prepared to make a defense to anyone who asks you for a reason for the hope that is in you."* (1 Peter 3:15)

Hope. What is my hope? Why do I believe what I do? That is what Peter is saying I need to answer for, when asked. I do not have to know everything about the Christian faith. I do not need to know where the remains of Noah's ark are, what happened to the dinosaurs, or who the Antichrist may be. I only need to have a reason for *my hope*. That is exactly why my boys need to take my faith, but then make it their own. Their hope will be different than mine. Yes, I absolutely hope part of their faith story will include Amber and me and the work we are doing to grow our sons' faith. But, at some point, they have to make it their own.

I need to help them make it their own. I need to help them

know how to study. I need to teach them the importance of prayer. I need to help them know how to discern the will of God.

In doing all that, they start by taking my faith and then adapting the faith to be their own.

Professing and Possessing

As I think about my boys taking my faith and making the Christian faith their own, I want them to also profess the faith, and truly possess it. This idea comes from a section of scripture found in Matthew 7:21-23. Jesus is near the end of his most famous teaching, the Sermon on the Mount. He just finished talking about the Golden Rule and trees that produce bad fruit.

He then says, *"Not everyone who says to me, 'Lord, Lord,' will enter the kingdom of heaven, but the one who does the will of my Father who is in heaven. On that day many will say to me, 'Lord, Lord, did we not prophesy in your name, and cast out demons in your name, and do many mighty works in your name?' And I will declare to them, 'I never knew you; depart from me, you workers of lawlessness.'"*

Whoa. Those are some harsh words from Jesus. But he is clearly calling on us to do more than simply profess Him as Lord.

Anyone can profess Christ. They can even do great works in His name. I firmly believe that my boys could say they are Christians, go to church their whole lives, and still be outside the kingdom of heaven. This is what would happen if my boys were to simply take my faith, but not make it their own.

Jesus is clear that His followers will know Him. They will hear Him, and listen to Him (John 10:27-28). They will have a relationship. They will spend time together. This means having a daily quiet time (DQT) where His followers read and pray. I need to invite my boys into my DQT so they see it, take it, make it theirs, and then truly possess it for themselves.

The Christian faith is more than something to just profess. Saying it is not enough. In fact, only saying it really does not matter at all. In order for the faith to be real, one must possess it. One must hold it so tightly it looks like ownership of the faith. This is the kind of faith I want for my boys.

You Root for Who?

Now, let me give you the perfect example of how something important can be handed down to our boys and become something they make their own and deeply possess.

I have some friends who are Cleveland Browns fans.[2] The Browns have been around since 1946. They last won the Super Bowl in 1964 and, as of August 2018, they hold the longest active playoff drought. They have not been to the playoffs in the last 15 seasons. How could anyone be a Cleveland Browns fan?

Well, my friends will tell you they have been Browns fans their whole lives and grew up in a family that always rooted for the Browns. They will tell you about sitting around the radio and TV on Sunday afternoons, while their dad and grandpa yelled with such passion you would have thought the players could hear them. They will tell you about the first time they went to a home game and saw the *Dawg Pound*, a bleacher section famous for its devoted fans.

---

[2]The Browns are a professional American football team. I use the word "professional" loosely.

My friends can relay the roster of every team they have ever seen play. They would be able to describe memorable moments with such heartbreak you would think the fumble had happened to them. Yesterday. They can recount, with tears in their eyes, the dark years of '96 through '99 after Art Modell moved the team to Baltimore.

They will then share, exuberantly, exactly where they were when they heard the Browns were coming back to Cleveland. They can show you pictures of their kids wearing Browns gear as babies and of them, thrilled, taking their son to his first game.

This is what taking/making and professing/possessing look like in the world of sports. If you are Browns fan, you get it.[3] You completely understand how something so important to your dad is ingrained in who you are. Now you cannot wait to share it with your son and help him find the joy of fandom.

The mindset of a father who is a Cleveland Browns fan is the mindset a Christian father needs for his son. With the same intentionality, the Christian father must point his son to Christ.

The son must first take his father's faith. His father must help the son make it his own. The son must decide to do more than profess that faith; he must possess it for himself.

---

[3] Fans of the Carolina Hurricanes, Sacramento Kings, Seattle Mariners, and dozens of other perennial losers get it, too.

DEAR BOYS EXTRA
Four Rules for Getting Boys to Take the Faith

There are countless books about how to get kids to take the faith and I certainly encourage you to read them. There are experts who write, teach, and speak on the topic all the time; listen to them. Here are four things from my experience with my four boys that I believe you can do to help ensure you sons take your faith and make it their own.

1. Make it a priority – They will value what you value. Attending church regularly must be a priority. There should never be a Sunday where you "just don't feel like going," so you skip it. Do not put them into a travel sports league where you will constantly miss church. I know, you have paid a lot of money, they are good at it, and they don't want to miss out. May I just say that if you had that mindset towards your faith (put money into to, get good at, don't miss out), you would want to be at church on Sunday. Do not prioritize anything over Sunday morning.

2. Worship together – When you go to church, if your child is in middle school or high school, have him sit with you. I do not believe that kids 12+ should be doing their own thing on Sunday morning. They need to see what the body of Christ looks like, worshipping together. If not, they will never actually feel like part of a church, just a youth group. I want them to love being part of the body, so when they leave my home, they will want to be part of a body wherever they are.

3. Be in community – Beyond Sunday morning, be part of a small group of some kind. Your boys need to see you block time on your calendar to spend with other believers on other days. Small group community is where the Church really comes alive. It is where we care, pray for, and love each other. It is where we can challenge each other and grow. Your boys need to see you in community.

4. Let them be in community – For all the reasons listed above, your boys need to be in community as well. Find a good youth group where they will be taught, challenged, loved by others, and hang with friends. Community will always be important. Give them the opportunity to experience it now.

Breakfast Discussion

QUESTIONS FOR DADS:

1. Share your testimony as a Christian with your son.

2. What do you really hope your son knows about Christ?

3. What do you need to do in your own life to grow your faith?

QUESTIONS FOR SONS:

1. By watching your dad, how important would you say his faith is to him?

2. If you have claimed Christ as your Savior, what is your hope for your faith?

3. As you prepare to leave home, what do you need to do to ensure your faith is yours, and not simply the one your parents want you to have?

QUESTION FOR BOTH:

What is the one thing from this chapter that stands out to you and what will you do differently in the future?

Sentence Ten

YOUR REMINDER

*I love you, am proud of you,
and I always have been.*

The Only Words That Matter

This chapter could easily have been rolled up into the previous one. The idea behind the last 12 words of my letter is a simple one.[1] As I talked about Grace and unconditional love, these 12 words are the embodiment of what that Grace looks like.

I wanted to have them stand alone in their own chapter, just as I want them to stand alone as a powerful end to a heartfelt letter.

Why? Because these are the 12 words I wish I was better at saying to my boys every day.

I love you, am proud of you and I always have been.

I believe these are phrases that our boys need to hear every day. These are the answers to the questions our sons are asking, deep down in their souls. With every word and action, what they really want to know is if we love them and are proud of them. Saying these words to our boys fills a hole in their psyche they may not even realize exists.

True Love

I tell my boys I love them all the time; I am sure you do, as well. But we must say the words consciously, sincerely and with intent. We must not say them by rote; we can't just let them just be something recited without thought or emotion.

We get in the routine of walking out the door and saying, "Love you."

---

[1] That means this chapter will not be very long, so hang in there! I won't drag it out. Promise.

We tuck them in at night and say, "Sleep tight. Love you."

It becomes so routine I assume their "Love you, too," is nothing more a than muscle memory response.

Take time. Stop what you are doing, look at them, and tell them how much you love them. Often. Say it in a way that is different than how and when you usually say it. Catch them off guard. Let them hear the emotion in your words and see it in your eyes.

I firmly believe we cannot tell our sons enough that we love them.

Love them for who they are, regardless of what they do.

Remember Grace?

Pride

When was the last time you talked about your sons and were moved to tears because you just couldn't help yourself? It does not happen a lot in my life, but when it does, it is when I am talking about how proud I am of who they are as young men. When I have baptized them, I can barely speak.

They need to hear we are proud of them when they succeed. They need to know how much we admire their effort and their success. Think about how much we appreciate it when our achievements are recognized. Praise is exactly what our sons want from us, too!

More important than recognizing their successes, though, is that they know we are proud of them when they try, but fail. Just as my love is unconditional, my pride in who my sons are and the efforts they make is unconditional as well. Can I be disappointed in behaviors and decisions? Sure, I can.

However, that doesn't change the pride I have in them as my sons. They can never fall so far they lose my love or my pride in being their father.

Never Enough

"I love you," and "I am proud of you," can never be said enough to our sons. It is why those words make up the last sentence of my letter. I want them to know it was the last thing on my mind as I wrote it. I might not have saved the best sentence for last, but I certainly saved the most important.

If you cannot remember the last time you told your son you love him or are proud of him, do me a favor. Make a commitment right now that before you go to sleep tonight, you will tell him. In person, over the phone, in a text message, email, or letter—it matters not. Do not let another day go by without telling him.

If it is the first time you are telling him, it will take courage. Summon it. I promise he will remember it. I recall exactly where I was the first time I have a conscious memory of my dad telling me. I was seven years old and, looking back, I know my dad had just become a Christian and quit drinking. We were halfway up the long driveway to my grandparents' house. My father stopped the car, turned around toward the back seat and said, "You two boys know how much I love you, don't you?"

I have no idea how I responded (probably "Yeah"), but I will never forget hearing him utter those words. Those words from a father to a son are powerful, life changing, and life giving.

Do not ever let a day go by without telling your son that you love him and are proud of him!

Breakfast Discussion

QUESTIONS FOR DADS:

1. What do you love about your son?

2. Talk about why you are proud of your son.

QUESTIONS FOR SONS:

1. What do you love about your dad?

2. Talk about why you are proud of your dad.

QUESTION FOR BOTH:

What is the one thing from this chapter that stands out to you and what will you do differently in the future?

Your Turn

Your Turn

*The time for action is now.
It is never too late to do something.*
ANTOINE DE SAINT-EXUPERY

*There is something you must always remember.
You are braver than you believe, stronger than
you seem, and smarter than you think.*
A. A. MILNE

It Is Time

There we have it. My letter, explained.

I hope that as you spent time with your son going through this book, you had some great conversations. I hope you learned some things about him and see him differently. I hope he has learned some things about you and sees you differently!

My prayer is you have been challenged to look at what you have been chasing up until now and make a decision to chase something different. In the opening chapter, I said some of you will read this book and bemoan the fact that you didn't read it earlier.

Remember: it is never too late. Regardless of your son's age, it is never too late to write him a letter in the spirit of mine. I promise that if you take the time to write it and give it to him, it will change him.

It will change you.

You now have a choice. You can file this book away as an interesting read with some unique thoughts or you can pick up a pen and start writing. You can go back to being an engaged father or you can become an intentional father.

In this moment, the words of A.W. Tozer come to mind: "*Refuse to be average. Let your heart soar as high as it will.*"

There are no more breakfast questions. Instead, I have a simple template for you to use to draft your own letter. Use it to create your sentences. Do not get hung up on how many words you write. Do not worry if you combine some sections and only have seven sentences, or if you happen to have 15 sentences. What you write is infinitely more important than how many words or sentences you use.

If you do not like my template, do not use it at all! Sit down with a blank piece of paper and start drafting.

I ask only one favor. Please continue to share your success, as you have been, so we can cheer you on. On the morning you read your son your letter, post a picture using #dearboysbook![1]

I am humbled that you have read along and let me accompany you on your dad journey. But I am more humbled by the effort I know you are now going to make as you write a letter to your son.

It will change your life.

It will change his life.

It will change your family's legacy.

I am proud of you and with you all the way!

---

[1] I want other men to know they are not alone on this journey and in this effort!

Writing Your Own "Dear Boys" Letter

Use this template to write out your sentences. Once you are happy with them, write them out on a single piece of paper to give to your son. Spend time reflecting on what is most important to you. Share from your heart. Speak from your soul.

Dear Boys,

Your Guide (Use an opening sentence that gets their attention and lets them know you have something very important to share with them):

_____

_____

_____

_____

_____

_____

_____

_____

_____

_____

_____

Your Mom (Tell them what you want them to know about their mom and what you hope they will do for her when you are not around):

Your Manhood (Share your definition of Manhood):

Guides (Let them know you have men who will be there to help them; list those men if you want):

Your Job (Tell them what you expect from them when you are gone regarding loving and leading their siblings, their own kids, etc):

Your Wife (Share with them what it means to you for a husband to love and lead his wife):

Your Savior (Point them to the power of the Cross and Jesus Christ):

Your Reminder (Share some final words with them—the most important words):

Love,
Dad

Acknowledgments

This book has been on my heart for a long time, so to see it finally happen is a dream come true. As with most dreams that come true, it could not have been realized without countless people having my back and holding me up.

To my wife, Amber: Thank you for your support during this process. I know I would not be the man and father I am today without you in my life. You have made me a better person in so many ways. No marriage is perfect, but we struggle for each other daily. Thank you and I love you.

To my parents: When I first told you we were having a son, you said, "Good. That's what you deserve." I had no idea what you meant, but I do now! While my childhood had its ups and downs, I know you always did the best you could. That is all any person can ask for and I hope my boys see the same commitment in me. Thank you for a home where humor, sarcasm, and movie quotes always kept us laughing.

To my test readers: Your feedback, insights, and questions made this a better book. Thank you for taking the time to share.

To my editor, Susan: Thank you for your dedication and professionalism. There is no one else I would rather have work on my books. You make me look good!

To Doug, Lauren, John, and Katie: Your creativeness and generosity took what was in my head and put it on the cover. Thank you!

Finally, to my boys, Evan, Joah, Owen, and Liam: I love doing life with you all. Thank you for putting up with me, teaching me, and offering me forgiveness when I don't get it right. I love with you all my heart.